THE
WHISKEY
COMPANION
A CONNOISSEUR'S GUIDE

by
HELEN ARTHUR

THE
WHISKEY
COMPANION

A CONNOISSEUR'S GUIDE

by
HELEN ARTHUR

RUNNING PRESS
PHILADELPHIA · LONDON

A QUINTET BOOK

9 8 7 6 5 4 3 2 1
Digit on the right represents number of this printing.

Library of Congress Control Number: 2007929449
ISBN: 978-0-7624-3006-2

Project Editor: Marianne Canty
Designer: Rod Teasdale
Editorial Assistant: Robert Davies
Art Director: Sofia Henry
Managing Editor: Donna Gregory
Publisher: Gillian Laskier

This book may be ordered by mail from the publisher.
Please include $2.50 for postage and handling.
But try your bookstore first!

Running Press Book Publishers
2300 Chestnut Street, Philadelphia, PA 19103-4371

Visit us on the web!
www.runningpresscooks.com

Picture credits: all bottle images by kind permission of the manufacturers and distillery owners. Additional images: Bruichladdich Distillery Co (p.6); Buffalo Trace Distillery Inc (p.13); John Dewar & Sons/Bacardi (p.27); Duncan Taylor & Co (p.3); Glenfarclas/J&G Grant (p.2, p.8, p.22, p.23); Grant & Sons (p.7, p.14, p.21); Highland Park Distillery/Edrington Group (p.9); Laphroaig/Fortune Brands (p.1, p.4, p.25); Morrison Bowmore (p.11, p.15, p.16, p.17, p.18, p.19); Penderyn Distillery/ Welsh Whisky Co (p.12); US National Archives (p.11); Wild Turkey Bourbon Distillery/Pernod Ricard (p.20). Images on p.24 taken by Nick Wright. Additional thanks to The Whisky Exchange, London.

CONTENTS

INTRODUCTION

My grandparents thought you shouldn't love food, only people. I don't know why, but this was one of those late Victorian maxims in which they believed. I am not sure what they would make of my abiding love affair with whisky. Not that I drink vast quantities you understand, but I am passionate about discovering more concerning the history of whisky, the people who make whisky, and every day I learn something new. I am consistently surprised at the differences to be discovered in a glass of whisky; the nuances of color, viscosity, flavor, aroma, and mouthfeel. It is even more surprising when you consider that they all have three key ingredients in common — grain, yeast, and water. Of course there are variations because of the different types of grain used and the methods of distillation vary from distillery to distillery and from country to country. Then when you introduce a fourth ingredient — peat — new dimensions of color, taste, and smell appear.

At first glance it all seems very simple, but clearly it isn't. In the following chapters I will introduce you to "my wonderful world of whisky." Not only how it is made, with some ideas on why each whisky is so different from its neighbor, but also an insight into the history of some of the world's leading brands.

Space does not permit an in-depth study of all the whiskies of the world, this book is therefore an overview of some of the most well-known brand names and an introduction to some of the new kids on the block. Please accept my apologies if your favorite has been omitted. Single malts and blends are featured from Scotland, but of course there are also some single grain bottlings such as Girvan, Invergordon, and North British, which are worth tasting if you can find them in your local store.

Since I wrote *The Single Malt Whisky Companion* in 1996 a great deal has changed in the whisky world. United Distillers and IDV have become Diageo, Allied Distillers has been sold to Chivas Pernod Ricard of France and Fortune Brands of the United States, Glenmorangie is now part of the luxury goods empire LVMH. Some distilleries have closed for ever, elsewhere dustcovers have been taken off distilleries, equipment refurbished, and new owners have breathed life into them.

All over the world, interest in single malts, small batch Bourbons, and other specialty whiskies has increased. New distilleries are springing up everywhere, often very small, but others are very big indeed. For instance on February 15, 2007 Diageo announced they were investing £100 million and building a new malt distillery in the north of Scotland.

This enthusiasm for fine whiskies has brought about changes in the way they are produced. Improvements are being made and fewer factories are creating spirits from sugar or other distillates and labeling them whisky. Counterfeits especially of premium brands are still a major problem and passing off dubious spirits as whisky is still prevalent in some parts of the world. However the tight regulations surrounding whisky production, for example, in Scotland, are being replicated globally. This is very good news for the consumer.

I could not have written this book without the support and friendship of a very large number of people in the whisky industry. They are far too numerous to mention, and I hope they will understand and accept my grateful thanks for everything.

A FEW IMPORTANT NOTES

- All of the distillery names and brand names mentioned in this book are registered trade marks.

- All of the information is, I believe, correct at the time of going to press. I can only apologize for any mistakes or if telephone numbers and other details have changed in the meantime.

- The pictures have been provided by the companies concerned and are subject to international copyright and must not be used without their permission. A list of picture credits is given on the copyright page.

- I have called bottlings, which have more than one single malt in them, Blended Malts instead of Vatted or Pure Malts, as I think this makes things clearer and hopefully will avoid confusion.

- The word whisky is usually used in Scotland, Canada, Japan, and many other parts of the world. Whiskey is more usual in Ireland and the United States, but as you will see there are some exceptions to this rule.

WHERE DID IT ALL BEGIN?

A display set up at Glenfarclas to pay tribute to the old illicit distillers.
The actual still in the picture is genuine, but customs and excise
have cut the base out of it so it cannot be used.

The history of whisky is shrouded in mystery. It appears that the earliest distillers were the Chinese and the knowledge was then passed on to India, the Middle East, and beyond. Pliny the Elder described basic stills for the creation of turpentine from rosin in 23-79 AD. The Egyptians were distilling wine and herbs in the third century AD, and in the 10th century apothecaries in Salerno, Italy, working at the medical school developed medicines distilled from wine, cereal, or herbs. It is believed that the distillation of alcohol did not start until the eleventh century when equipment was developed to cool the vapor rising up the still so that it could be converted back into liquid form.

Scotland

The first written record is in the Scottish Exchequer Rolls for 1494 with a reference to "eight bolls of malt to Friar John Cor wherewith to make aquavitae." A boll is equivalent to approximately 330 pounds (150 kilograms).

The first reference to a Scottish distillery is made in 1690 when the name of Ferintosh distillery, Culloden, appears. However, it is clear that some 50 years before, many farmers were distilling whisky on a commercial scale; in 1644 the Scots Parliament passed an Excise (Customs Duty) Act raising duty on "aquavitae" and other strong alcohol of 2/8d per gallon.

Distillers only attracted duty if they were selling their whisky. Production initially centered on local communities where resources were shared. The temptation to distil more to gain additional income meant that production increased and sales were made outside the neighboring area. Other sources believe that production increased because being a distiller was more prestigious than being a farm laborer. By 1579 there were a large number of distilleries in Scotland. Up to the end of the seventeenth century most of the distilleries were small concerns. There is one common thread throughout the following centuries — distilling attracts taxation.

In 1707, following the Act of Union, the government tried to bring the taxes raised in Scotland into line with English taxes, which did not meet with general approval. The 1736 Gin Act was designed to curb excessive drinking in England and did not apply to Scotland. This had the effect of increasing Scottish production of *uisge beatha* (whisky) and not unsurprisingly much of the spirit was destined for the English market. Distilleries, especially Lowland ones with easy access to road transport, grew in size as a result.

The year 1756 was exceptionally bad for grain harvests, and as a result distilling was banned, essentially until 1760. This ban only applied to licensed stills and not to private distilleries whereby households could distil for their own purposes. The following years were colored by the introduction of numerous Acts; some had the desired effect of legalizing distillation in one area, only to encourage illegal activity in another. Evading the taxman became a national sport, particularly in the Highlands of Scotland.

The Highland Park Distillery is still producing single malt whisky to this day.

Milton Duff distillery is situated in the Glen of Pluscarden, where the surrounding hills form a triangle. The local distillers devised a warning signal. A flag was raised on one of the hills to warn of the approach of customs and excise officers. A conscientious exciseman learned of this practice, however, and hid all night until the men were in the fields. He arrived at the farmhouse to find the farmer's wife dismantling the still. She was apparently a very sturdy woman; he was much smaller. Legend has it that he was never seen again.

While distilleries could be dismantled and hidden, stocks were not so easy to hide. There is a tale which relates how Magnus Eunson, the distiller at Highland Park in Orkney, who was also the local preacher, used to hide barrels of whisky in his church. On hearing that the excise men were in the area, the barrels of whisky were taken from the church and hidden under a white cloth in his house. While the excise men searched the church, Eunson and his staff placed a coffin lid under the cloth and started a funeral service. One of the employees whispered that smallpox had been the cause of death and this was enough to make the excise men flee in terror.

The Lowland distilleries struggled after the introduction of the Lowland Licence Act in 1788 designed to protect English distillers, and large concerns such as the Kincaple distillery, owned by Robert Stein, and Lochrin, owned by John Haig, got into difficulties.

By the end of the eighteenth century there were two distinct types of spirit produced in Scotland — malt, which had achieved a following of its own; and grain, much of which was destined for rectification by gin distillers. Malt was produced primarily by small Highland and Island distilleries, much of it illegal, and grain by licensed large-scale Lowland distilleries, although there were clearly exceptions to both.

In 1823 following a Royal Commission, the Excise Act was introduced, which encouraged distillers to obtain a license. Duty was reduced, but penalties for unlicensed premises were severe. The first to take out a license with the support of his landlord, the Duke of Gordon, was George Smith of The Glenlivet. As described in the Single Malts Chapter, John Smith of Glenlivet's decision to go legal in 1824 did not meet with his neighbor's approval. By 1825 there were 263 licensed distilleries and many distillers were slow to follow his example. A large number of Scotch malt whisky distilleries operating today date from this period.

The majority of sales were made in bulk to distributors and retailers, who were responsible for transferring the whisky to bottles for sale to the public. Many of these retailers were to become leading lights in the industry, especially with the introduction of blended whiskies; Chivas Brothers, Arthur Bell, William Teacher, Johnnie Walker, and John Dewar. However, at the lower end of the market, mixing whisky with other products to make it go farther was common practice, as noted in a Select Committee Report of 1855.

To create a brand required careful supervision of the finished product and also a consistency in quality, flavor, and color. This is difficult as no two casks are ever the same, as described in the chapter on how whisky is made. For this reason, distillers always marry a selection of casks to create their "signature malts." Early retailers were totally reliant on the distillers, many of whom cut corners, and it was only when the retailers themselves could build up sufficient stocks that quality could be assured. Andrew Usher was the first to publicize this in 1821, and by 1860 he had developed the art of marrying, in particular casks of The Glenlivet, so that he could launch the first branded whisky, Usher's Old Vatted Glenlivet.

Whisky achieved kudos in the eyes of the general public following Queen Victoria's interest in all things Scottish. The demise of the Cognac industry following the destruction of the European vineyards (1879-1886) through the introduction of the Phylloxera vine louse also provided a boost to Scotch whisky.

Distillers were looking at ways of creating a still which would provide a quicker, continuous method of distilling. The first was invented by Robert Stein of Kilbagie distillery in 1827. Aeneas Coffey's still, which he invented in 1830, was an improvement on the earlier Stein still. By 1860 Coffey had refined his still using copper for the analyzer sections rather than wood, and this is still used today. The creation of blends using a mixture of single malts and grain whisky led to an overall improvement in the finished product.

This was a huge period of growth in the Scotch whisky industry and, as will be seen later in the book, blenders such as William Teacher, George Ballantine, Johnnie Walker, and the Chivas Brothers were major contributors. Single malts were only promoted by a few companies until 1963 when Glenfiddich started marketing their brand.

Today 10,000 people are directly employed in Scotch whisky production and 41,000 jobs in Scotland depend upon the industry.

Around the World

The first stories relating to whisky distilling in Ireland date from the twelfth century. Whether this was as a result of monks or soldiers traveling there with the knowledge or not is unclear. There is also nothing to disprove the theory that farmers discovered the art for themselves as a means of using surplus barley. There are stories of King Henry II's army drinking whiskey in the late twelfth century when fighting with the King of Leinster and taking some back to England with them. At Bushmills, Sir Thomas Savage reputedly sent his men into battle after giving them whiskey to drink in 1276. But this is only hearsay and there is nothing written down to prove or disprove these stories.

In its heyday there were more whiskey distilleries in Ireland than in Scotland. Before Prohibition, Irish whiskey was the favorite drink in America. When Prohibition was introduced the Irish appeared to acquiesce; they didn't seek to

Detroit police inspecting equipment found in a clandestine brewery during the Prohibition era.

smuggle their whiskey in through the numerous "back doors" used by the Scotch whisky industry. Unfortunately many bootleggers passed off their spirits of dubious quality as Irish, which did the real thing untold harm. The Irish whiskey industry never really recovered, even after the Volstead Act repealed Prohibition. At the same time in Ireland, the Irish were seeking Home Rule and this meant that they lost the lucrative English and British Commonwealth markets.

Today, there are just four distilleries left, Bushmills in Northern Ireland, Cooley, Kilbeggan (which started again in 2007 after a long period of inactivity), and Midleton.

Wales is not a country which readily springs to mind when talking about whisky, but some of the key distillers in America such as Jack Daniels, Evan Williams, and Elijah Craig, were of Welsh origin. Elijah was a Baptist minister and farmer who started distilling in America in the late eighteenth century. I have not looked

The modern Penderyn Distillery bottling line bringing whisky production back to Wales.

deeply into the history of Welsh distilleries, but it ceased totally in 1900 when the Bala Distillery closed. There have been several attempts to revive the tradition in recent times, but it was only in 2000 that whisky started to run from a Welsh still again at Penderyn distillery.

The fact that whisky is now produced around the world has led me to carry out some research. From this I have made a few conclusions, which could well be erroneous but are in my view interesting. For example, there seems to be a correlation between the fact that Scots engineers traveled the world constructing bridges, laying railroad tracks and roads, with the appearance of distilleries. In some instances the dates do support this hypothesis, for example in India the Indian East Coast Railway was completed in 1850. The Kasuali distillery at Solan, 90 miles (150 kilometers) from Simla, which was built by a Scot, Edward Dyer, has a mash tun dated 1855 and the original copper stills were made in Scotland. A friend of mine visited the

distillery in 2007 but unfortunately it was closed. There are now a large number of distilleries in India producing a wide variety of blended whiskies and a few single malts.

In New Zealand the first recorded whisky distillery opened in Cumberland Street, Dunedin in 1867. Dunedin was established as a Scottish Free Church Settlement in 1848. The South Island Main Trunk Railway linked Dunedin with Christchurch, and in the City's charter of 1865 spirits and beer were listed among other products manufactured in the area. A second distillery opened in Auckland and the railroads provided the distillers with access to a large percentage of the population. These early distilleries were, however, forced to close under pressure from the Scotch whisky producers who were afraid of losing one of their more lucrative overseas markets. In time, however, whisky distillation was revived but is still in its infancy.

The Japanese whisky industry was developed by Masaraka Taketsuru who worked at several distilleries and attended Glasgow University in Scotland in 1918. Taketsuru returned to Japan in 1920 along with his Scottish wife and started working for Shinjiro Torii of Suntory, who wanted to build a whisky distillery in Kyoto. Taketsuru left Suntory in 1930 to found Nikka. Today Japan is a key producer of both fine single malt and grain whiskies.

American whiskey started with the immigrant settlers who came from England, Ireland, Scotland, Wales, Germany, and Holland, who not only brought the knowledge of how to produce, but also a fondness for spirits.

Distilling began in Pennsylvania and Maryland and spread south; for example, records show that whiskey was first made in Leestown, Kentucky around 1787. As in Scotland, the early distillers were seen as targets for taxation and their refusal to pay taxes in 1791 fueled the Whiskey Rebellion of 1794. The distillers in Pennsylvania refused to pay the tax, and President George Washington sent in 13,000 troops to quell the rebellion. As a result thousands of Scottish and Irish immigrants moved from Pennsylvania into the Ohio River Valley. They arrived with their stills loaded onto boats and settled in Kentucky.

Early distillers chose to create their whiskeys from local corn instead of using the traditional rye and barley. Today Bourbons such as Buffalo Trace Kentucky Straight Bourbon use selected corn, rye, and malted barley to create their signature bottlings. Dr. James Crow emigrated from Scotland to Woodford County in Kentucky. He developed a more accurate way of controlling fermentation and also urged distillers to mature whiskey to improve its flavor.

To return to the railroad theme, distillers in America used this form of transport in the early days. The most famous American whiskey bridge crossed the Kentucky River close to Wild Turkey, which at the time of writing is unsafe to use. A few companies still use the railroad for collection and distribution, such as Jim Beam's Clermont distillery.

The American Civil War (1861–1865) meant that many distilleries closed down, and the end of the war was a period of renewal and growth. Production increased considerably and some of the distilleries were very big enterprises. The introduction of Prohibition in 1920 forced many distilleries to close. Prohibition lasted until 1933 – by this time the face of the American whiskey industry had changed forever. Today, key players are once again producing, and investment in new plants has been made at some distilleries, but production is a long way off from the heady days of the late nineteenth century.

Buffalo Trace Kentucky Straight Bourbon aging in a warehouse dating from 1885.

PRODUCTION PROCESSES

To make whisky you need grain, yeast, and water. To make a single malt you need malted barley, yeast, and water. These are the key ingredients, but there are variations and these help distillers create Irish whiskeys, Bourbons, and other distinctive whiskies.

This apparently simple recipe belies the complexity of the finished products.

At the beginning of the separate chapters covering Irish, American, and Canadian whiskies some of the key differences in the production process are discussed.

Making Single Malt

Water The starting point is a pure, clean, continuous water source. In Scotland, as the water tumbles down from the Scottish hills or across peat bogs to the distillery, it will carry with it a little of its birthplace. Distillers believe that the fact that their water source is hard or soft is important to the composition, aromas, and flavors of the final product. For example, at The Glenlivet Josie's Well provides the water, which is mineral rich and enables the distillery to "extract sugars more easily from the malt." For this reason I wrote in Whisky, Uisge Beatha

— The Water of Life, "The water source, whether it is alkaline or acid, hard or soft, plays an important part in the taste and smell of the final single malt."

However, there is a school of thought, which says the part water plays in the final product isn't as important as I suggested. The view is that a large proportion of the minerals dissolved in the water are lost through distillation. This may be true, but I still believe that enough local water characteristics remain and can be identified in single malts.

Barley The type of barley is carefully selected by the distillery managers. There are specific strains of barley developed by farmers and agronomists for distilling. The malster looks for barley with a low nitrogen content, which is crucial for good fermentation, and a moisture content of no more than 16%, so the barley will be ripe and dry when it leaves the fields. In the silo the barley will dry to a moisture content of 10–12% and will enter a period of dormancy which will last approximately 8 to 10 weeks before the barley can be malted.

Converting Barley to Malted Barley

The grains of barley are soaked in water for a couple of days until the moisture content has reached approximately 45%; then the barley is either spread out on a traditional stone malting floor or transferred to drum or Saladin maltings. The barley will start to grow; rootlets and a shoot will appear on each grain and soluble starch will be produced, which will convert into sugar during the mashing process.

Drying the Malt The next step is to dry the malt. Traditionally, the malted barley was removed from the malting floor and then transferred to the kiln where it was spread out over perforated metal or tile floors above a peat fire. Peat impregnates the barley with its characteristic smoke taste and aroma. In the past most distilleries used peat, but as coal became more freely available with the growth of the railroads, mainland production changed, creating less smoky whiskies. On islands such as

Islay and Skye, the transition to coal did not happen quickly and the use of peat continued. For most island whiskies this is still the norm, whether traditional kilns or larger maltings are used to dry the barley.

In the case of the larger commercial maltings where Saladin boxes or drums are used, warm air created by using gas or oil burners is blown through the barley. The barley is rotated to ensure even drying. Where an element of peat smoke is required, this will be included to achieve a particular distillery's "recipe." The amount of smoke used will vary and this is measured in phenol parts per million.

In Scotland four distilleries produce 100 percent of their own malting supply, but only two do this in the traditional way. The biggest and certainly the oldest among them is Springbank, which supplies maltings for distillations of Springbank, Longrow, and Glengyle. The other and much smaller is the new kid on the block, Kilchoman on Islay.

After steeping in water, barley is spread out on a traditional stone malting floor to germinate.

Mash tuns, which are usually made from copper, are used to extract the sugars from the malt grist.

At Balvenie 10 percent of the total requirement, and at Bowmore, Laphroaig and Highland Park 20 percent of the total, is produced using traditional floor maltings. At Tamdhu 100 percent of their supply is made using Saladin box maltings, and at Glen Ord 100 percent is produced using both Saladin and drum maltings for Glen Ord itself and six other Diageo distilleries. There are a few distilleries with traditional malting floors such as Glendronach and BenRiach, which have not been used for a long time.

Otherwise, maltings are carried out at larger maltings throughout Scotland. It is possible to tour some of these, and one of the most frequently visited must be Port Ellen on Islay, which provides malted barley for the seven major distilleries on the island.

Mashing After a rest period the dried malt is ground to a fine grist in a malt mill. The grist is composed of flour and solids including the grain husks. The grist is transferred to a mash tun with hot water between 145°F and 154°F.

Mash tuns vary in size and shape, but are usually made of copper and have a lid. The hot water dissolves the flour and the starches in the malted barley have converted to sugar. The liquid or mash is turned mechanically inside the mash tun and the liquid is drawn through the base of the finely slotted base. The liquid then passes into an underback and more hot water is added until all the sugars are extracted from the grist. The final water will be kept and added to the hot water used for the next mashing.

The hot sugary liquid is known as wort and this passes through a refrigerator to cool it down to about 72° to 75°F. At Edradour there is an original Morton cooler similar to ones formerly used in farm dairies. In most distilleries the refrigerator is a paraflow plate heat exchanger. The liquid is then transferred to fermentation vessels or washbacks. The solids (known as draff in Scotland) which remain are removed from the mash tun and used as cattle feed.

Fermentation Washbacks are traditionally made of Oregon pine, although there are a few distilleries with stainless steel washbacks in Scotland. Interestingly, Bowmore changed to stainless steel, but after a time switched back to wooden ones. Yeast is added to the washbacks and fermentation will start. The yeast converts the sugars into alcohol and congeners, such as esters, aldehydes, and acids. The wort will produce carbon dioxide and will start to foam. To stop the foam pouring over the sides of the washbacks, switchers are used to break it down. Once fermentation has stopped, a malt ale is produced. The time will vary depending on the size of the washback, but is usually a couple of days. The malt ale will be between 5%–10% alcohol and is known as wash.

Distillation The wash is transferred into a wash charger and will then be pumped into the still room. Stills are made from copper and vary in size and shape. Copper is a soft, pliable material and in time the stills wear away, especially where the spirit comes into contact with the sides.

Stills normally operate in pairs; one wash and one spirit still. The wash is first pumped into the wash still. The still is heated to a little below 212°F and as the temperature rises the alcohol will start to turn into vapor and rise up the still into the neck and through the lyne arm into a worm or condenser to be cooled. The first coolers were called worm tubs and were made from coiled copper piping. At the end of the nineteenth century a shell-and-tube condenser was invented which uses less water and is easier to clean. Worms have the effect of making a heavier spirit, and among those which still use a worm tub are Balmenach, Mortlach, Royal Lochnagar, and Talisker.

The liquid which is created after the alcoholic vapor (known as low wines) has passed through the condenser is collected and then transferred to the spirit still. The low wines are heated in the spirit still, which is usually smaller than the wash still. The condensed vapors will pass through a spirit safe. All spirits are subject to customs duty in the United Kingdom and indeed many other countries, and the spirit safe is locked to ensure that exact measurements are taken of the spirit produced.

The first spirit is known as foreshots and this will pass from the glass bowls in the spirit safe to a collecting tank. The foreshots turn cloudy when they come into contact with water as they are still impure. The stillman watches the spirit safe very closely at this stage and when the correct purity and specific gravity are reached, the middle cut is collected and stored in a spirit receiver. Dependant upon the speed of distillation but usually after a couple of hours, the stilllman will divert the spirit flow, known as feints, to the low wines tank. For example at Ardbeg the foreshots run is about 15 minutes, spirit is taken off for approximately 3 hours and the feints run is another 4 hours.

The malt ale, or wash, is passed through two sets of heated copper stills.

It is only the middle or spirit cut which is passed into a vat and subsequently to casks for maturation.

This is true of all single malt distilleries in the United Kingdom, with several notable exceptions, for example Auchentoshan and Bushmills, where the spirit is triple distilled before being transferred to casks for maturation.

Maturation Spirit comes off the still at around 67% and is clear and colorless. It is this spirit which needs to mature for a minimum of three years in oak casks before it can be called whisky in Scotland. Testing new spirit can be a real adventure for every distillery's output is different. It is surprising how soft and creamy some new spirit is and how the aromas and flavors, which will be found in the finished product 10 years on, can be detected. Maturation has to be the most magical part of whisky production for no one really knows what goes on inside the cask.

Distillery managers exercise stringent control to ensure that the spirit is carefully measured as it is piped into barrels for maturation and the total volume recorded. All whisky warehouses are bonded; that is they hold goods in bond so that the appropriate amount of duty is paid at the time of bottling.

Most Scotch whisky companies use a mixture of barrels, predominantly ex-American Bourbon casks and Sherry butts. As wood is permeable, the air surrounding the barrel will seep into the whisky and spirit will seep out of the barrels, this is known as the "angels' share." The thought of drunken angels flying over distilleries has to be a happy one. The temperature and humidity of the warehouse will affect the speed of maturation. The longer a malt whisky is left to mature in the barrel, the more changes will take place, which is why malts of varying ages from the same distillery can differ from one another.

The barrels are checked constantly to ensure that everything is well and that the whisky is sleeping happily.

Once the optimum level of maturation has been reached, the whisky is removed from the cask for bottling. In some instances, the whisky will be taken from one cask and transferred to another for secondary maturation or finishing. The choice of second cask is wide and growing, for example you can find whiskies which have been finished in Port Pipes, Madeira Casks, various types of Sherry butts (e.g. Oloroso, Pedro Ximenez), wine casks (e.g. Bordeaux, Tain L'Hermitage, Sauternes), or Cognac barrels.

To illustrate how maturation affects a single malt, here are details of a vertical tasting I attended on May 24, 2003 at Lagavulin distillery with the then manager, Donald Renwick. We started from new make to 25 years and my notes are as follows:

The stillman monitors the spirit safe closely to determine when the correct purity is reached.

New spirit matures for a minimum of three years in specially selected casks.

"The journey from new make with the peaty, oily elements you would expect was very interesting. At 3 years old the wood took over, at 5 years the phenols were back and at 12 years a good combination was in place of wood and peat phenols. The 5 year old was malty, coriander notes were prevalent with the smoke and peat really hitting. At 12 years old honey, caramel and fruit (bananas) mixed with the smoke and there's a creamy dry finish. At 16 years the malt is instantly recognisable and it is truly the signature Lagavulin, there's still caramel and vanilla but the fruit is more currants with spice and there's smoke and peat to produce a well balanced harmonious whole. The 25 year old was less recognisably Lagavulin with more fruit and less peat."

Casks were used from the very beginning of whisky production, as they provided an easy means of transporting the new spirit, although it is uncertain when the idea of maturing whisky first started. In the history of The Glenlivet there is a reference to the fact that when George IV visited Edinburgh in 1822 he was given some Glenlivet whisky by Elizabeth Grant of Rothiemurchus. In her memoirs she wrote, "My father sent word to me — I was the cellarer — to empty my pet bin, where there was whisky long in the wood, long in uncorked bottles, . . . " This is, I believe, the first time maturation is mentioned.

The art of cask making or coopering is very old; the Worshipful Company of Coopers (Coopers Guild or Trade Association) was registered in London in 1501. It is not the oldest Company; for example, the Barbers started in 1308, Brewers in 1437, and Carpenters in 1333. It was not until 1638 that the Distillers Company was founded. The Barbers Company was known as the Barber-Surgeons from 1540-1745. It is interesting to note that the Scottish Guild of Surgeon Barbers in Edinburgh was created in 1506 and they were granted the monopoly for the manufacture of aqua vitae (whisky) within the Burgh of Edinburgh.

Making Grain Whisky

The process is relatively similar to that for producing single malt whisky. In the past the whisky was distilled in large pot stills in the Lowlands of Scotland. Today grain whisky is created in large patent stills, invented in the 1820s. The majority of these grain or patent stills follow the original designs of Aenas Coffey, an Inspector General of Irish Customs and Excise. The stills are tall, comprising two columns, a rectifier and an analyzer. They distil quickly and continuously and are relatively cheap to run. The final spirit is purer than single malt spirit and can be much stronger — up to 94%. The pureness of the spirit makes it ideal to mix with single malts to create blends.

The mash in a grain distillery will consist of a mixture of malted barley, unmalted grain, and cooked maize.

Again, the spirit must be matured for at least three years in the United Kingdom before it can legally be called whisky.

Making Irish Whiskey

Irish whiskeys are produced in the same way as single malts and grain whiskeys. However, there are various styles of Irish whiskeys, which set them apart from standard blended whiskies. Irish pot-still whiskey is made from a mixture of malted and unmalted barley. Irish whiskey, with no other definition shown on the label, is a blend of grain, malt and pot-still whiskeys. By varying the proportion of each ingredient it is possible to create a wide variety of whiskeys. For example, at Midleton they create more than 30 different whiskeys.

Making Bourbon Whisk(e)y

By law, Bourbon must be pure, created only from water, grain, and yeast and matured in wood with no additives or coloring. There must be a minimum of 51% corn, and the other grains can be rye, wheat, and malted barley. Bourbon is very much part of America's history. One of the very first distillers was George Washington.

Bourbon distillers talk of cooking the whiskey, whereas in Scotland they talk about mashing, but from that point on the terminology is the same; fermenting and distilling follow, then maturation in oak casks. However, there is a distinct difference between cooking and mashing, as the milled grain is mixed with water and placed in steam-powered pressure cookers for about an hour. At Buffalo Trace, for example, the ground corn is initially cooked and then as the mixture cools, rye and malted barley slurry is added. The malted barley converts the starches in the cooked grains into soluble sugars.

American whiskeys use new American white-oak barrels, which have been charred on the inside. This releases the tannins and vanillins in the oak, which enhance the raw spirit to produce fine balanced whiskeys. Maturing Bourbons is a skilled art as the cold winters and hot summers mean that the whiskeys are alternately cooled and heated. Warehouses are traditionally built of brick with earth floors, and the barrels stored on racking typically six floors high. Each distillery will create its own cycle of movement within the warehouses and have identified the floors which produce the best whiskies.

Charring the white-oak barrels at the Wild Turkey Bourbon Distillery.

TASTING WHISKY

When we talk about tasting whisky, we really mean nosing, tasting, and looking at whisky. For the enjoyment of discovering and appreciating a glass of whisky uses all of our senses.

The first thing to say is please take time. Tasting is a leisurely activity to be enjoyed either alone or with a special group of friends. Make sure you have plenty of glasses (you will need a different one for each whisky), pure water, either from your own well if you are lucky enough to have one, or bottled still water. Water which has been treated with chlorine will alter the characteristics of the whiskies and will not allow you to make a clear judgement.

The key element that makes one glass of whisky different from another is the way in which it is produced.

Is it a single malt? If so then the differences will be determined to some extent by the type of barley used, whether the barley has been dried using peat smoke or not, and many distillers believe the type of yeast used introduces subtle changes to their whisky. The size and shape of the copper stills make a difference, and if a worm tub is used to condense the vapor, the additional time in contact with the copper affects the final spirit. The judgement and skill of the distillery staff at each stage, including choosing the cut off points when taking the spirit off the stills, will influence the whisky. Finally, and most importantly, the type of cask used for maturation and the length of time in the cask characterizes the spirit.

If the whisky is a blend, then you will not necessarily be able to learn much from the label; but there will be clues, such as whether or not there is an age declared. Some companies state that their blend has a high volume of malt compared to grain whisky in the blend, others state that the blend is in fact pure malt only.

For Bourbon whiskeys the method of production is not dissimilar to single malt but there are key differences. For example, the label may show the words sour mash which denotes a stronger, sourer mashing process (please see the section on Bourbons, opposite, for more information). The grain used will certainly be corn or maize with a percentage of others such as rye, wheat, and barley; these will give different flavors to the finished spirit.

Another word of advice, please leave a little of each whisky in your glass, so that you can revisit them again. You will be surprised by the changes in aroma and taste.

Tasting a Single Malt

When presented with a glass of whisky for the first time, do not drink it straightaway. First, look at the glass — hold it up to the light. If it is a dark copper color it has probably been matured in a first fill Sherry butt. By first fill, I mean the first time that the cask has held whisky. Beforehand the butt will have contained Sherry which will have permeated the oak wood with color and flavor, which is then transferred to the new spirit.

If the color is a warm gold it could have been matured in a first fill Bourbon cask. Bourbon casks are often charred inside before the whiskey is placed inside to give it the distinctive Bourbon character.

When the whisky is a paler gold, then it is likely that the barrels have been used once before for maturation. If it is very pale then the casks could have been used up to three times, and then the terminology is that the whisky has been matured in plain oak.

By making these assumptions, we can guess how the whisky would smell and taste. A Sherry cask will probably impart a sulfur nose with caramel, spice, and rich fruit. A Bourbon cask could give the whisky more malt grain notes with vanilla, toffee, and lighter fruit flavors. These are not hard and fast rules and every whisky will have different aromas and taste, but this gives you an idea of what to expect.

Also swirl the glass around and the whisky will coat the inside of the glass. Hold the glass up to the light and you should see a curving line above the whisky. This line will have legs (these can also be called tears or Cathedral windows) running down. These legs may be running very

Hold the glass up to the light to assess both the color and "legs" of the whisky.

To nose the whisky, slowly move the glass under your nose — do not inhale too deeply.

fast and close together, which could denote that the whisky is young. If they are slower and wider apart then it is very likely that the whisky is older, and if the legs are oily and fat looking then the whisky is most likely a peated one. These are only pointers, but on the whole I have discovered them to be a reasonably good guide to the contents of the glass.

Now nose the whisky, please do not put your nose straight into the glass; all you will smell is spirit and you will experience a prickling sensation. Move the glass slowly under your nose from side to side, that way you should catch the aromas as they rise above the spirit. Then add a little water, just a drop and swirl the whisky around in the glass. There will be subtle changes in the aromas you are detecting; add a little more water and again the smell will alter as the spirit reveals itself.

The next thing to do is take a small sip and move the whisky around your mouth, almost chewing it and let it cover your tongue and the roof of your mouth. This will give you a clear indication of the body of the whisky, is it full-bodied or light? Is the whisky going to remain in the mouth for a long time or is it going to dance on your tongue and creep quietly away?

You may want to add a little more water at this stage to encourage additional flavors to identify themselves (but do not drown the whisky). As I go through these stages, I usually write down what I discover. With practice you will be able to identify more each time you nose and taste a whisky. Most of the time the nosing is a good indicator of what you should expect on the tongue, but there will be surprises. For example, sometimes the nose will be light and delicate yet in the mouth the whisky will be strong and full-bodied.

Then there is the finish. As you swallow the whisky you will notice that flavor elements are left in your mouth. If they disappear quickly, then this is described as a short finish. Alternatively they may stay for quite some time — a long finish.

And then go back to the first glass and just nose and taste again to see how the whisky has changed.

TASTING NOTES IN THE BOOK

For the most part the tasting notes in the book are my own. I have spent many happy hours often alone, sometimes with friends, looking at, nosing, and tasting these whiskies. I choose to do my tasting early in the day when I believe my nose and palate are at their best. Clearly this is only possible when you are lucky enough to be working from home as I do and haven't anywhere to drive to later in the day!

I have chosen words to describe the color, aroma, and flavors which I hope convey my thoughts clearly and concisely. Use my notes as a guide to help you discover other elements in each whisky. In several instances I have not been able to taste the whiskies, so there are no tasting notes. For a few whiskies I have included notes provided by the company or my business partner Caroline Dewar.

Assess the color of the whisky.

Swirl the whisky to release the aroma.

Cover the glass to contain the aromas.

Gently nose the whisky.

Slowly sip the whisky.

SCOTCH WHISKIES

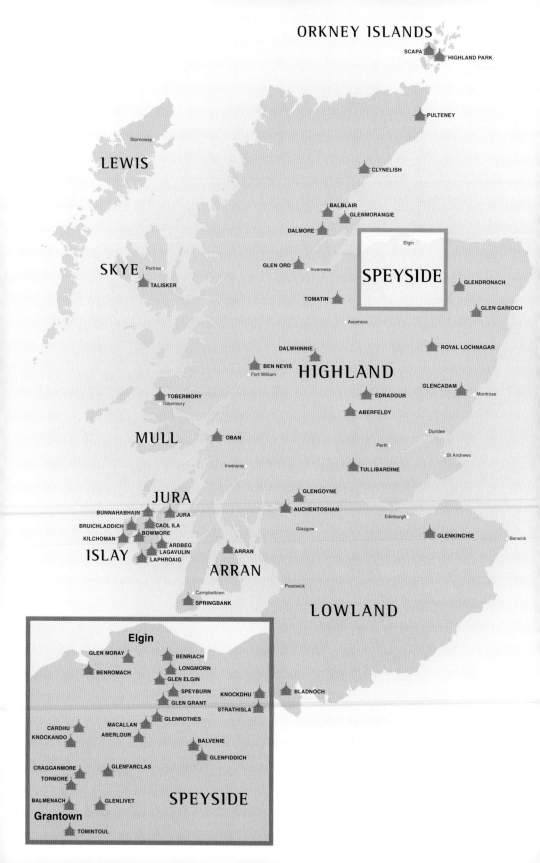

ORKNEY ISLANDS

SCAPA
HIGHLAND PARK

PULTENEY

Stornoway

LEWIS

CLYNELISH

BALBLAIR
GLENMORANGIE
DALMORE

Elgin

GLEN ORD
Inverness

SPEYSIDE

GLENDRONACH

SKYE
Portree
TALISKER

GLEN GARIOCH

TOMATIN

Aviemore

DALWHINNIE
BEN NEVIS
Fort William

ROYAL LOCHNAGAR

HIGHLAND

GLENCADAM
Montrose

TOBERMORY
Tobermory

EDRADOUR

ABERFELDY

MULL

OBAN

Dundee

Perth

St Andrews

Inveraray

TULLIBARDINE

JURA

GLENGOYNE

BUNNAHABHAIN
JURA
BRUICHLADDICH
CAOL ILA
KILCHOMAN
BOWMORE
ARDBEG
LAGAVULIN
ISLAY
LAPHROAIG

AUCHENTOSHAN

Edinburgh

Glasgow

GLENKINCHIE
Berwick

ARRAN

ARRAN

Prestwick

Campbeltown
SPRINGBANK

LOWLAND

Elgin

GLEN MORAY
BENRIACH
LONGMORN
BENROMACH
GLEN ELGIN
SPEYBURN
KNOCKDHU
BLADNOCH
GLEN GRANT
STRATHISLA
GLENROTHES
CARDHU
MACALLAN
KNOCKANDO
ABERLOUR
BALVENIE
GLENFIDDICH
CRAGGANMORE
GLENFARCLAS
TORMORE
BALMENACH
GLENLIVET
SPEYSIDE
Grantown
TOMINTOUL

SINGLE MALT SCOTCH WHISKIES

Single malts are largely responsible for the almost frenetic interest in whiskies around the world. This is a relatively recent phenomenon. When whisky was first produced in Scotland at small farm distillers, only single malts were available and most were drunk locally. As whisky's fame spread and production increased, small casks were illegally carried on donkeys over secret pathways to the nearest towns.

The invention of the Coffey still — which produces grain spirit — and the art of blending brought whisky to a much wider audience. From the mid-nineteenth century onward the emphasis was on selling blended whiskies. There were, of course, exceptions to this generalization, such as Gilbey's Strathmill, which was sold as a single malt in the 1900s. However, it wasn't until 1963 when William Grant & Sons decided to actively promote their single malt, Glenfiddich, separately that interest was revived. Since then the market sector has exploded, although it should be said that single malts still only account for some nine percent of the world's whisky sales.

Whisky production has not really changed in the intervening years, and single malts are still produced at individual distilleries using time-honored traditional skills. Whisky is no longer consumed straight from the still and now spends years carefully maturing in oak casks, so that the spirit mellows and takes on the color and flavors of the wood.

Some distilleries have been looking to the past and have revived old recipes. For example, Glenfiddich Caoran Reserve was developed in recognition of the peat legacy found in casks distilled in the 1930s and 1940s. The advent of coal meant that peat was no longer used for fuel. However due to a shortage of coal during World War II a greater percentage of peat was added to the maltings fire to ensure continuing production at the distillery.

Other companies are reviving old distilleries. In March 2007, Bruichladdich announced their intention to start rebuilding Port Charlotte and new stills will be installed soon. The distilling equipment is from the Inverleven Distillery demolished in 2003.

ABERFELDY

Highland

Aberfeldy Distillery
Aberfeldy, Perthshire PH15 2EB
Tel: +44 1887 822010
www.aberfeldy.com / www.dewarsworldofwhisky.com

OWNERS: JOHN DEWAR & SONS/BACARDI

FOUNDED: 1896

VISITOR CENTER: YES

Aberfeldy was built in 1896 by John and Tommy Dewar, on the south bank of the River Tay. Aberfeldy takes its water from the Pitilie burn, which served a former distillery that closed in 1867.

Aberfeldy is the signature malt in all of Dewar's blends. In 1890 A. J. Cameron joined Dewar's and he developed the art of pre-vatting malt and grain whiskies until they had reached the optimum for blending. Aberfeldy distillery gave Cameron the heather honey notes ensuring all Dewar's blends would reflect those originally designed by John and Tommy Dewar.

Aberfeldy closed during World War I as the government restricted the use of barley for food production. The distillery reopened in 1919, was purchased by Distillers Company Limited in 1925, and closed again during World War II until 1945. In 1998 Bacardi bought John Dewar & Sons from Diageo. Aberfeldy's visitor center is now Dewar's World of Whisky.

Aberfeldy 12 year old was introduced in 1999 and Aberfeldy 21 year old launched in 2005.

ABERFELDY 12 YEAR OLD 40% (80°)

Color   Warm honey gold.

Nose   Honey, malt, clove spice, lush.

Taste   Light smoke, burned sugar, creamy mouthfeel with a long vanilla honey finish.

ABERFELDY 21 YEAR OLD 40% (80°)

Color   Light honey.

Nose   Initially spirity, malty, with water opens to reveal burned caramel and dried fruits.

Taste   Dry, roasted nuts, licorice, medium-bodied with a long, dry finish.

ABERLOUR

Speyside

Aberlour Distillery
Aberlour, Banffshire AB38 9PJ
Tel: +44 1340 881249
www.aberlour.com

OWNERS: CHIVAS BROTHERS PERNOD RICARD

FOUNDED: 1879

VISITOR CENTER: YES

Aberlour is Gaelic for the "mouth of the chattering burn." The distillery sits below Ben Rinnes near the Linn of Ruthie which tumbles 30 feet (9 meters) into the Lour Burn. There is a well fed by a spring in the grounds dating back to when the valley was occupied by a Celtic community established by St. Drostan.

Aberlour was founded in 1879 by James Fleming, who also owned Dailuaine. In 1898 fire almost destroyed Aberlour — Charles Doig, who designed over 100 distilleries in Scotland and Ireland, helped redesign the distillery.

After various changes of ownership, Pernod Ricard purchased Aberlour in 1975. Aberlour is the leading single malt in France and available worldwide. The visitor center opened in 2002 and visitors can fill a bottle of whisky straight from the cask.

Aberlour 10 year old, 12 year old Double Cask Matured, 16 year old Double Cask Matured, 12 year old Sherry Cask Matured, 15 year old Double Cask Matured and a'bunadh (Gaelic for "of the origin") are available.

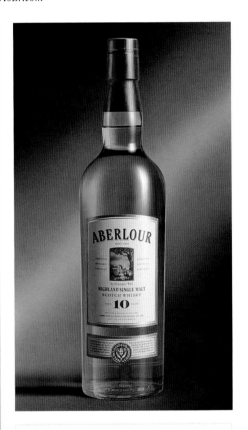

ABERLOUR 10 YEAR OLD 40% (80°)

Color   Amber gold.

Nose   Heady malt, citrus, honey, and light smoke.

Taste   Medium-bodied with hints of peat and honey, dry finish.

ABERLOUR 12 YEAR OLD
DOUBLE CASK MATURED 43% (86°)

Color   Warm gold with copper highlights.

Nose   Light caramel, malt, chocolate, and fennel.

Taste   Luscious, full bodied, oak, toasted almonds and caramel, coats the mouth with flavor. Warm, ripe, honey with a hint of licorice finish.

ARDBEG

Islay

Ardbeg Distillery
Port Ellen, Isle of Islay, Argyll PA42 7EA
Tel: +44 1496 302244
www.ardbeg.com

OWNERS: THE GLENMORANGIE CO (MOËT HENNESSY)

FOUNDED: 1815

VISITOR CENTER: YES

Sitting on the ferry from the mainland the first buildings you notice as you approach Islay are the whitewashed distilleries of Kidalton and to your right is Ardbeg. The ninth century Kidalton Cross erected by monks who escaped from Norse invaders on Iona is nearby. Distilling started on the island in the sixteenth century and there was a distillery on this site by 1794. Today's distillery dates from 1815 when John MacDougall built Ardbeg. In 1853 John's son, Alexander, who was running the distillery by then, died and his sisters Margaret and Flora took over the licence with Colin Hay. By 1886 Ardbeg was employing 60 people from a village population of 200. After the sisters' death Colin Hay and Alexander Buchanan became owners of the distillery.

The distillery was purchased by Hiram Walker and Distillers Company in a joint venture company. Ownership changed when Allied Lyons bought Hiram Walker in 1987. The latter years were bad for Ardbeg, it closed in 1981 and reopened only for short periods until 1996 when the distillery was closed and put up for sale by Allied Distillers.

The new owners Glenmorangie plc knew they had a distillery capable of making one of the world's most famous peaty single malts, but the buildings and equipment were in a very sad state of repair. The task, to an outsider certainly, seemed a very daunting one. Ardbeg has literally been reborn to worldwide acclaim. The visitor center with its excellent restaurant is always packed and Ardbeg's bottlings are collector's items.

ARDBEG TEN YEARS OLD 46% (92°)

Color   Pale gold.

Nose   The first elements are peat smoke and wild honey then dark chocolate and scents of the sea.

Taste   The smoke and honey on the nose mingle in the mouth with sweet orange, malt and chocolate. A long, smoky slightly sweet finish.

AIRIGH NAM BEIST 1990 46% (92°)

Color   Pale gold.

Nose   Initially a one-dimensional smoke punch, then hints of salt spray, a medicinal nose.

Taste   Heather honey, shortbread, green pepper and smoke. A surprisingly short medium sweet finish.

ARRAN

Isle of Arran/Highland

Arran Distillery
Lochranza, Isle of Arran KA27 8HJ
Tel: +44 1770 830264
www.arranwhisky.com

OWNERS: ISLE OF ARRAN DISTILLERS

FOUNDED: 1993

VISITOR CENTER: YES

The isle of Arran is situated on the west coast of Scotland close to the Kintyre peninsula. Harold Currie dreamed of building his own distillery and on retirement from Chivas chose Arran to realize his vision. On August 17, 1995 distilling was reborn after 158 years when the first spirit ran from the stills. The last Arran distillery closed in 1837.

Today visitors to the island drive to the village of Lochranza on the island's northern coast to Arran distillery. Apart from seeing how this single malt is made, there is a great restaurant, which has become a favorite with locals and tourists alike.

The distillery came of age on June 29, 2005 when the company bottled its first Arran 10 year old. That day something special happened, for eagles were seen soaring above Goat Fell just behind the distillery, just as they did when the first stones were laid in 1993.

Some young whisky has been transferred to other casks for secondary maturation. Finishes to date include Sauternes, Bourgogne, Cognac, and Port casks. It has been a privilege to watch Arran grow and the 10 year old certainly, to my mind, fulfils the distillery's earlier promise.

THE ARRAN MALT 10 YEAR OLD
46% (92°) NON-CHILL FILTERED

Color   Pale gold.

Nose   Light honey, summer sunshine, and hayfields. The spirit aromas have gone, which were prominent in earlier bottlings.

Taste   Light creamy mouthfeel, summer blossoms, vanilla honey with a dry, medium finish.

THE ARRAN MALT SAUTERNES FINISH 56%
(112°)

Color   Light mahogany.

Nose   Raisins, caramel, malt, hint of salt, and smoke.

Taste   The first notes are dry with a hint of peat, in the mouth opens out to dried fruit, caramel with a dry, spiced finish.

AUCHENTOSHAN

Lowland

Auchentoshan Distillery
Dalmuir, Dunbartonshire G81 4SG
Tel: +44 1389 878561
www.auchentoshan.com

OWNERS: MORRISON BOWMORE

FOUNDED: 1823

VISITOR CENTER: YES

Visitors on their way from Glasgow to Loch Lomond and Islay, pass Auchentoshan distillery; visible from the Erskine Bridge. The distillery sits close to the River Clyde with the Kilpatrick Hills rising on the other side. The name Auchentoshan is "corner of the field" in Gaelic and the distillery still sits in a patch of green, but Glasgow continues to grow and there are housing estates close by, so the city is gradually creeping ever closer.

The distillery was built as Duntocher in 1800, but was not licensed until 1823. There were several changes of ownership until 1941 when the distillery was damaged in a German bombing raid. The owners, Maclachlans Ltd, did not start rebuilding until 1948. The distillery was bought by Tennent's, the Scottish brewer company, in 1960 and then in 1969 sold to Eadie Cairns. In 1984 Stanley Morrison bought the distillery from Eadie Cairns Ltd.

Auchentoshan is the only Scottish malt to be regularly triple distilled. In the past most Lowland distilleries were produced in this way.

Auchentoshan is one of the few Lowland distilleries still operating today; the others are Bladnoch and Glenkinchie. The earliest Lowland distillery started in 1741 and well over 200 distilleries operated throughout the region during the nineteenth century. Many of them produced grain whisky and spirit which was sent to England for rectification into gin.

AUCHENTOSHAN SELECT 40% (80°)
Tasting notes courtesy of Morrison Bowmore.

Color   Pale straw.

Nose   Floral, green apples, and a hint of lime.

Taste   Soft blackcurrant and lime flavors, a touch of aniseed and malty sweetness with a short, soft, and fresh finish.

AUCHENTOSHAN THREE WOOD 43% (86°)

Color   Bright sunshine gold.

Nose   Full big impact nose, which initially hides the normal Auchentoshan light scented, citrus notes.

Taste   The wood elements are the first flavors to come through, caramel, candied orange, toasted nuts, tobacco, and a long finish.

BALBLAIR

Highland

Balblair Distillery
Edderton, Tain, Ross-shire IV19 1LB
Tel: +44 1862 821273
www.balblair.com

OWNERS: INVER HOUSE DISTILLERS

FOUNDED: 1790

VISITOR CENTER: NO

Founded by John Ross, Balblair lies just north of Glenmorangie and is one of the oldest operational distilleries in Scotland, although it has moved from its original site. In 1824 John Ross's son Andrew started working at Balblair, but in 1834 moved to run Brora. In 1836 John died and Andrew, with his sons, moved back to Balblair. Andrew didn't relinquish the license at Brora until 1846. Andrew died in 1873 and his son James carried on the business. James moved the distillery on the Balnagowan Estate closer to the railroad track.

In 1911 the distillery closed and by 1932 there was no stock left. The Balnagowan Estate was sold off in 1941 and the distillery was purchased by Robert Cumming. Distillation started again in 1948 and in 1970 the distillery was bought by Hiram Walker. In 1996 Inver House Distillers purchased the distillery from the owners Allied Distillers.

Whisky production was erratic in the past and for many years nothing was distilled. Inver House purchased some stock with the distillery and special releases have recently been introduced. Balblair is now distilling and new bottlings are eagerly awaited.

BALBLAIR 1979 VINTAGE 46% (92°)

Color   Pale summer gold.

Nose   Light malt with summer fruits, hint of caramel, and vanilla.

Taste   Medium-bodied with caramelized fruits, light spice, and a dry light slightly bitter sweet finish.

BALBLAIR 1989 VINTAGE 43% (86°)

Color   Pale gold and green straw.

Nose   Old leather, malt, and almonds. With a little water opens up to include toffee, unripe pears, and a hint of citrus.

Taste   Complex flavors with hints of dried fruits, lemon peel, and a dry finish.

THE BALVENIE

Speyside

Balvenie Distillery
Dufftown, Keith, Banffshire AB55 4DH
Tel: +44 1340 820373
www.thebalvenie.com

OWNERS: WILLIAM GRANT & SONS

FOUNDED: 1892

VISITOR CENTER: ONLY OPEN TO PREBOOKED GROUPS

Balvenie was built alongside Glenfiddich distillery by William Grant and both distilleries still belong to the same family. Balvenie is one of the few distilleries to still have its own floor maltings, which provides 10 percent of the total requirement.

The Balvenie was first launched as a single malt in 1973 and in 1982 The Balvenie Founder's Reserve was introduced.

One key topic of conversation in recent years has been the subject of finishing whiskies or giving them a period of secondary maturation in a different cask. Sometimes whisky has to be moved from one barrel to another, for example because the original has sprung a leak – this is known as re-racking. The second cask would normally be as close to the original as possible.

In 1982 David Stewart, William Grant's Master Distiller, transferred The Balvenie into a Sherry cask, but this change of cask was not shown on the label. However, in 1993 David introduced The Balvenie DoubleWood, which is matured in traditional oak and Sherry casks and in 1995 The Balvenie PortWood was released.

The standard expressions for The Balvenie are Founder's Reserve 10 years, DoubleWood 12 years, and PortWood 21 years. Other special bottlings are released occasionally.

THE BALVENIE FOUNDER'S RESERVE
10 YEAR OLD 40% (80°)

Color   Pale summer gold.

Nose   Light smoke with citrus and a hint of honey.

Taste   A dry, refreshing malt with a rounded taste, sweetness from the Sherry casks and a hint of smoke, a lingering finish.

THE BALVENIE DOUBLEWOOD
12 YEAR OLD 40% (80°)

Color   Warm honey gold.

Nose   Gloriously rich, crystallized fruits, Sherry notes, and caramel.

Taste   Full-bodied, layers of flavor, first notes are caramel and fruit, then there's a hint of dry, toasted hazelnuts with nutmeg and Sherry, smooth on the palate with a sweet finish.

BEN NEVIS

Highland

Ben Nevis Distillery
Lochy Bridge, Fort William PH33 6TJ
Tel: +44 1397 702476
www.bennevisdistillery.com

OWNERS: BEN NEVIS DISTILLERY LTD
(NIKKA, ASAHI BREWERIES)

FOUNDED: 1825

VISITOR CENTER: YES

Ben Nevis is the only distillery to obtain its water from Britain's highest mountain. Built in 1825 by John Macdonald, known as "Long John," whose name is still linked with whisky today. The *Illustrated London News* for April 1848 records a visit by Queen Victoria to Fort William and that "Mr Macdonald has presented a cask of whisky to Her Majesty and an order has been sent to the Treasury to permit the spirits to be removed to the cellars of Buckingham Palace free of duty. The cask is not to be opened until His Royal Highness the Prince of Wales attains his majority."

John died in 1856 and his son Donald Macdonald took over Ben Nevis at the age of only 20. He was very successful and opened a new distillery, Nevis (or Glen Nevis), which operated from 1878 to 1908. This Glen Nevis distillery should not be confused with the distillery of the same name, which was founded in 1877 in Campbeltown and closed in 1923.

D. P. McDonald & Sons sold both distilleries to Joseph Hobbs, a Canadian who owned Bruichladdich, Glenesk, and Glenury Royal in 1941. The story goes that he immediately sold Nevis Distillery to the neighboring Glenlochy Distillery for warehousing, but took the gates and walls from Nevis and installed them at Ben Nevis. They are still there but they do not fit, as they were meant to be installed elsewhere. The bonded warehouses of Nevis distillery are still used by Ben Nevis. Ben Nevis was purchased by Nikka in 1989.

BEN NEVIS 10 YEAR OLD 46% (92°)

Color   Bright gold.

Nose   Warm, honeyed with citrus, dried fruits, and malt.

Taste   A full-bodied malt with Sherry notes, warm fudge, and a coating oily mouthfeel with smoke leading to a dry, slightly bitter finish.

BENRIACH

Speyside

Benriach Distillery
Elgin, Morayshire IV30 8SJ
Tel: +44 1343 862888
www.benriachdistillery.co.uk

OWNERS: THE BENRIACH DISTILLERY COMPANY LTD

FOUNDED: 1898

VISITOR CENTER: NO

BenRiach distillery was founded in 1898 by John Duff and Company, who started Longmorn distillery less than a quarter of a mile away. The two distilleries were originally linked by a railroad track, and the company's own steam locomotive "The Puggy" transported coal, barley, peat, and barrels between them. BenRiach is Gaelic for "the Hill of the Red Deer" and is in the heart of the Speyside region. BenRiach distillery only produced whisky for a couple of years as the Pattison brothers' scandal meant that John Duff had to sell his company. In 1899 the bank sold BenRiach to the Longmorn Distillers Company, but it was mothballed by 1903 and only the maltings continued to produce malted barley for Longmorn.

It was not until 1965 that the distillery reopened, and in 1978 Seagram Distillers purchased BenRiach. In 2004 the distillery was sold by then owners Chivas Brothers Pernod Ricard to Billy Walker, a former director of Burn Stewart and Intra Trading of South Africa.

The new owners have released a wide range of BenRiach expressions including "Heart of Speyside" unaged, BenRiach 12 year old, BenRiach 16 year old, BenRiach 20 year old, and two peated versions — BenRiach Curiositas 10 year old and BenRiach Authenticus 21 year old. From time to time the company also issues special expressions such as BenRiach 15 year old Pedro Ximenez Finish, which are nonchillfiltered and bottled at 46%.

BENRIACH 16 YEAR OLD 43% (86°)

Color   Warm golden sunshine.

Nose   The first notes are sweet summer honeysuckle, apple blossoms, and vanilla then elements of malted barley and oak wood emerge.

Taste   Well rounded rich, honey and vanilla notes on the tongue as well as orchard fruits and caramel.

BENRIACH CURIOSITAS 10 YEAR OLD 43% (86°)

Color   Deep amber gold.

Nose   Intense aromas of peat smoke and grass with hints of honey and fruit.

Taste   Smoke on the tongue with hidden notes of malt and light caramel.

BENRIACH 15 YEAR OLD MADEIRA FINISH (HENRIQUES & HENRIQUES CASK) 46% (92°) NONCHILLFILTERED

Color   Warm light mahogany.

Nose   Pear drops, dry, barley, celery, and vanilla.

Taste   A creamy mouthfeel, light caramel, dried apricots, and spice with a dry finish — a perfect after-dinner drink.

BENROMACH

Speyside

Benromach Distillery
Forres, Morayshire IV36 3EB
Tel: +44 1309 675968
www.benromach.com

OWNERS: GORDON & MACPHAIL

FOUNDED: 1898

VISITOR CENTER: YES

Benromach is near Forres and is the smallest working distillery in Speyside. The architect Charles Doig was responsible for building the distillery with its distinctive pagoda-style kiln chimney. At Benromach he also designed a recycling process for the water taken from the Mosset Burn, so that it was cooled and returned unpolluted. Duncan McCallum of Glen Nevis Distillery and F. W. Brickman, spirit dealer of Leith, Edinburgh were the first owners.

It closed in 1907 and reopened in 1909 as Forres, with Duncan McCallam still at the helm. In 1911 Harvey McNair & Co of London purchased the distillery but it closed in 1914 with the outbreak of World War I. In 1919 Benromach reopened but closed again in 1931. In 1937 distilling resumed and the following year Associated Scottish Distillers bought Benromach. Benromach then passed into Distillers Company ownership and was closed in 1983.

Gordon & MacPhail purchased Benromach in 1993 together with some stock. Everything inside the distillery is new including the two stills and larch washbacks. The distillery was reopened by HRH The Prince of Wales on October 15, 1998. Three rare Sherry casks, used since 1886, 1895, and 1901 were filled with 15 year old Benromach and released two years later to coincide with the distillery's centenary in 1998.

May 2004 saw the launch of Benromach Traditional; the first new single malt whisky to be distilled by Gordon & MacPhail. Benromach is also available as Benromach 21 year old and Benromach 22 year old Port Wood finish, with occasional special releases.

BENROMACH TRADITIONAL 40% (80°)

Color — Medium gold.

Nose — Distinctive light, hints of honey, and smoke.

Taste — Light-bodied malt with all the elements on the nose replicated in the mouth.

BOWMORE

Islay

Bowmore Distillery
Bowmore, Islay, Argyll PA43 7JS
Tel: +44 1496 810441
www.bowmore.com

OWNERS: MORRISON BOWMORE DISTILLERS

FOUNDED: 1779

VISITOR CENTER: YES

When I wrote my first whisky book, *The Single Malt Whisky Companion*, I spent a very happy day with Jim McEwan at Bowmore. There we discussed whisky for hours, tasting new make and different Bowmore expressions as we looked out across the bay. The newly refurbished visitor center provides similar views and a visit to Bowmore is a must.

If you want a swim while you are on Islay, the swimming pool is next door to Bowmore, located in one of the old warehouses and heated by recycled hot water from the distillery.

In 1766 David Simpson — a farmer, merchant, postmaster, and sailor — bought land from the Campbells to build a distillery, but there were protracted arguments over water rights. The first mention of Bowmore is in 1779 and it is the oldest distillery on Islay. After several changes of ownership, the distillery was bought in 1852 by William and James Mutter, who actively promoted the whisky as a single malt, particularly overseas. A Canadian advertisement shows a man drinking Bowmore with lemon and ice, not the usual thing today, but clearly popular at the time Stanley Morrison bought the distillery in 1963.

Bowmore operates its own floor maltings supplying 20 percent of its malted barley needs. The rest of its malt is obtained from Port Ellen on Islay.

On the November 16, 2006, Bowmore launched a "stunning new bottle, packaging and range" at the distillery on Islay. The core expressions include 12, 15, 18, and 25 year old Bowmore.

BOWMORE 12 YEAR OLD 40% (80°)

Color   Warm amber.

Nose   A light smoky nose with a stronger hint of the sea, citrus and heather notes.

Taste   The honeyed heather on the nose combines with the tang of the sea and peat smoke to produce round, satisfying flavors with hints of espresso coffee and a long finish.

BOWMORE 17 YEAR OLD 43% (86°)

Color   Deep honey gold.

Nose   The light smoke on the nose is wrapped around milk chocolate fudge.

Taste   Complex yet soft flavors of fudge with hints of smoke, cream, shortbread, and malt which fill the mouth. A warm, luxurious smoky finish.

BOWMORE 18 YEAR OLD 43% (86°)

Color   Copper with gold and auburn reflections.

Nose   The first elements are sweet, with plums, apricots, and other summer fruit, then the peat smoke starts to tickle your nose.

Taste   This is a complex single malt with the aromas replicating themselves in the mouth and a light smoky long finish.

BRUICHLADDICH

Islay

Bruichladdich Distillery
Isle of Islay, Argyll PA49 7UN
Tel: +44 1496 850 190
www.bruichladdich.com

OWNERS: BRUICHLADDICH DISTILLERY CO

FOUNDED: 1881

VISITOR CENTER: YES

The year 2000 saw the rebirth of Bruichladdich Distillery on Islay. Since 1994 its future has been uncertain and there were fears that it would be closed forever. But the doom merchants had not reckoned with the enthusiasm of a group of local businessmen spearheaded by Mark Reynier and Islay legend Jim McEwan. Jim had been persuaded to cross Loch Indaal and leave Bowmore distillery to reawaken Bruichladdich.

They bought the distillery and whisky stocks from Whyte & Mackay and started reviving "The Laddie." There was a considerable amount of work to do, stills and equipment were rusting away and buildings needed total refurbishment. The first spirit ran into the spirit safe at 8.26 a.m. on May 29, 2001. Bruichladdich has its own bottling line and is the only Islay distillery to do everything in-house.

A highlight of the annual Islay Music and Whisky Festival is Bruichladdich Day. The sun always shines, locals join the whisky aficionados from around the world, the bagpipes play, and everyone joins in the neverending "Strip the Willow" dance.

On August 29, 2001 the distillery launched its First Edition bottlings of 10, 15, and 20 year old single malts.

Bruichladdich is one of the least peated Islay malts and is noted for its fresh, honeyed, spicy flavors. In 2006 they launched 1,000 cases of a 5 year old Port Charlotte PC 5 Evolution, which is highly peated.

BRUICHLADDICH 10 YEAR OLD 46% (92°)

Color   Light with a hint of a new dawn sun.

Nose   Initially slight salt with warm Sherry notes then hints of citrus, summer blossoms – honeysuckle and apple.

Taste   The second fill Sherry casks come through quickly after the first dry sea air notes on the tongue. With water the taste expands with tangerine and vanilla cream from the Bourbon casks. A short, dry finish.

PORT CHARLOTTE 5 YEAR OLD PHENOL LEVEL 40PPMILLION MATURED IN MIX OF BOURBON AND SHERRY CASKS 63.5% (127°)

Color   Warm honey gold with hint of copper.

Nose   Malty sweetness, peat smoke, hints of the sea, musty hay, and caramel.

Taste   Burned caramel, dark chocolate, smoke, warm oily mouthfeel, and a dry malt and smoke finish. Already a good dram, there's promise of an exceptional, exploding, full bodied, peat and caramel whisky in a few years time.

BUNNAHABHAIN

Islay

Bunnahabhain Distillery
Port Askaig, Isle of Islay, Argyll PA46 7RP
Tel: +44 1496 840646
www.bunnahabhain.com

OWNERS: BURN STEWART DISTILLERS LTD

FOUNDED: 1881

VISITOR CENTER: YES

Distilling has been part of life on Islay for more than 400 years. Bunnahabhain is one of the most isolated and it is not hard to imagine life as it used to be on a farm distillery away from the eyes of the exciseman. Bunnahabhain was founded in 1881 by William and James Greenlees and William Robertson (Robertson and Baxter) and production started in 1883.

The distillery buildings form a square with a central gateway and a road, pier, and houses for the workforce and the customs and excise officer were also built. Bunnahabhain is Gaelic for "mouth of the river" and the River Margadale flows down into the bay alongside the distillery. There are four cottages at Bunnahabhain available for rent.

In 1887 the distillery merged with William Grant & Co to form Highland Distilleries Company Limited. The distillery closed in 1930, reopened in 1937, but closed again in 1982 to reopen in 1984. Edrington took over Highland Distillers in 1999 and production was restricted to a month each year. In 2003 the distillery was sold to Burn Stewart Distillers. The new owners are awakening this sleeping giant renowned for its lightly peated Islay malt. The distillery has experimented with more peated whiskies and the first limited edition 6 year old was launched in 2004.

Bunnahabhain is available at 12 years old and two new expressions, Bunnahabhain 18 year and Bunnahabhain 25 year. There have also been some special bottlings, for example a 14 year old Pedro Ximenez Finish.

BUNNAHABHAIN 12 YEAR OLD 40% (80°)

Color   Golden corn.

Nose   Definite aroma of sea and summer flowers with a hint of smoke.

Taste   Light and malty with a hint of peat, fills the mouth with a rich, lingering finish.

BUNNAHABHAIN 18 YEAR OLD 43% (86°)

Color   Bright mahogany light copper.

Nose   Burned caramel, raisins, and salted nuts.

Taste   First impressions are sweet caramel and dried fruits expanding to a rich dry nuttiness with hints of vanilla oak and spice. A perfect after-dinner drink.

CAOL ILA

Islay

Caol Ila Distillery
Port Askaig, Islay, Argyll PA46 7RL
Tel: +44 1496 302760
www.malts.com

OWNERS: DIAGEO

FOUNDED: 1846

VISITOR CENTER: YES

Caol Ila is Gaelic for the Sound of Islay, the stretch of water between Islay and Jura. Caol Ila faces Jura and one of the best views from any distillery has to be that of the Paps of Jura, as the mountains are called, from the still house.

The distillery was built by Hector Henderson in 1846. A waterfall supplied power, pressure for the fire hydrants, and water for whisky production. Henderson's business failed and Caol Ila was taken over by Norman Buchanan of Glasgow and the Isle of Jura distillery. In 1863 the distillery was purchased by Bulloch Lade & Co, who retain the licence to this day.

Alfred Barnard in his book *The Whisky Distilleries of the UK 1887* wrote "on the very verge of the sea . . . in a deep recess of the mountain, mostly cut out of solid rock, Messrs Bulloch Lade & Co. have built a fine pier at which vessels can load and unload at any state of the tide." For 100 years, barley from the mainland was brought by steamers or "Puffers" which returned with casks of whisky. In 1879 the distillery was rebuilt as the first concrete building on Islay.

After World War I, Bulloch Lade went into voluntary liquidation and after several changes of ownership Caol Ila was taken over by The Distillers Company in 1927.

The distillery was rebuilt in 1974. Billy Stitchell is the distillery manager. His father, grandfather, and great-grandfather all worked at Caol Ila. Caol Ila is used in many of Diageo's blends and bottled as a single malt.

CAOL ILA CLASSIC MALTS SELECTION ™
12 YEAR OLD 43% (86°)

Color — Pale straw gold.

Nose — Light honey, citrus, coal tar soap, and a hint of smoke.

Taste — Sweetness on the tongue at first then smoke bonfires, dry almost bitter, yet the heather honey note remains, with a medium finish.

CAOL ILA 18 YEAR OLD 43% (86°)

Color — Warm honey gold.

Nose — First vanilla, toffee, then mace, a malty mustiness, and a hint of blue cheese.

Taste — Light smoke. With water opening up to baked apple with cinnamon and spice and a creamy, sweet finish. This has to be one of my favorite expressions of this individual Islay malt.

CARDHU

Speyside

Cardhu Distillery
Knockando, Aberlour, Banffshire AB38 7RY
Tel: +44 1340 872555
www.malts.com

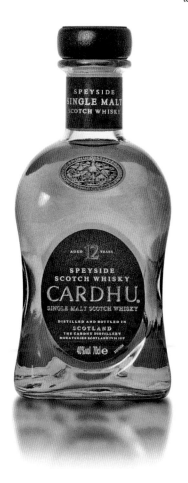

OWNERS: DIAGEO

FOUNDED: 1824

VISITOR CENTER: YES

John and Ellen Cummings farmed at Cardow and in 1813 they started distilling whisky, albeit illicitly. Customs officers visiting the Knockando area stayed at the farm. Ellen used to prepare a meal for the officers and once they were eating, she went outside and raised a red flag to warn other distillers that customs men were in the area. In spite of this, John had three convictions for distilling without a licence.

Cardow obtained a licence in 1824. In 1846 John died and his son Lewis took over the management of the farm and distillery. Until the Strathspey Railway opened, whisky was taken by horse and cart to Burghead and then shipped south to Leith. Lewis concentrated on producing good quality whisky and his brother James, a wine and spirit merchant in Edinburgh, was a key customer.

Lewis died in 1872 and his wife, Elizabeth, who was 24 years younger, was left in charge of the distillery. Elizabeth gained a reputation for her management skills and was nicknamed "The Queen of the Whisky Trade."

Cardow was bought by John Walker & Sons in 1893, the name was changed to Cardhu, and Elizabeth's son John was appointed a director. In 1908 the name reverted to Cardow and in 1925 John Walker and Son became part of Scottish Malt Distillers. The distillery was closed during World War II. In 1981 the name changed back to Cardhu.

Cardhu is the signature malt for Johnnie Walker blends.

CARDHU 12 YEAR OLD 43% (86°)
CLASSIC MALTS SELECTION ™

Color   Warm summer gold.

Nose   Summer on the nose with flowery notes – honeysuckle, sweet peas, and lemon blossom.

Taste   A light smooth whisky with honey tangerine, a creamy mouthfeel and a light silky finish.

CLYNELISH (& BRORA)

Highland

Clynelish Distillery
Brora, Sutherland KW9 6LR
Tel: +44 1408 623000
www.malts.com

OWNERS: DIAGEO

FOUNDED: 1819, REBUILT 1967

VISITOR CENTER: YES. RESTRICTED HOURS —
CALL DISTILLERY FOR OPENING TIMES

The story of Clynelish is of two distilleries and I include both here. The distillery was founded as Clynelish on land belonging to the Duke of Sutherland in 1819 by his son in law the Marquis of Stafford.

James Loch, the Marquis' Lands Commissioner wrote, "The first farm beyond the people's lot is Clynelish which has recently been let to Mr. Harper from the county of Midlothian. Upon this farm also there has just been erected a distillery at an expense of £750. This was done. . . to afford the smaller tenants upon the estate a steady and ready market for their grain without their being obliged to dispose of it to the illegal distiller."

James Harper started with one 200-gallon (908-liter) wash and one 87-gallon (363-liter) spirit still. In 1821-22 he produced 10,015 gallons (45,468 liters) on which he paid duty of £2,774. Andrew Ross took over the lease in 1834 followed by George Lawson in 1846. Ainslie & Co, Scotch Whisky Blenders bought the business in 1896. The Distillers Company took over the business in 1925. The distillery closed in the economic depression in the 1930s and again during World War II. In 1967 a new concrete, glass, and steel distillery was built next door. This was named Clynelish and the old distillery closed for a time. In 1975 it reopened as Brora and closed again in 1983.

Clynelish is available at 14 years old as part of the Classic Malts Selection. Special releases of Brora include a 30 year old in 2004 and another 30 year old in 2006.

CLYNELISH CLASSIC MALTS SELECTION ™
14 YEAR OLD 46% (92°)

Color — Warm honey gold.

Nose — Light smoke, scented apple blossom, malt, and green fields.

Taste — Medium bodied with a creamy texture in the mouth, on the tongue sensuous strands of sweetness and light smoke with a malty dryness and a hint of the sea. With water the flavors expand to include summer fruits. Dry, long, smoke finish with spice. A sexy dram.

BRORA 30 YEAR OLD 55.7% (111.4°)

Color — Amber gold.

Nose — Warm earth, wet leaves with a hot summer sun, light bonfire smoke, malt.

Taste — Honey, warm citrus, lemon and meringue pie, smoke in the back of the mouth, a long rounded finish.

CRAGGANMORE

Speyside

Cragganmore Distillery
Ballindalloch, Banffshire AB37 9AB
Tel: +44 1479 874700
www.malts.com

OWNERS: DIAGEO

FOUNDED: 1869

VISITOR CENTER: YES

Cragganmore was founded in 1869 by John Smith who was the most experienced distiller at the time. He was at Macallan in the 1850s, and then Glenlivet, Wishaw, and Glenfarclas distilleries. From Glenfarclas he persuaded his landlord, Sir George Macpherson Grant, to let him construct a distillery at Ayeon Farm. Smith chose the site carefully — he wanted to be the first to build a distillery close to the Strathspey Railway.

Cragganmore's layout today is relatively similar to that of 1869 according to a report in the local paper, the Elgin Courant, in June 1870. The majority was rebuilt in 1901 to the original layout.

John Smith was reputed to be a very large man weighing around 308 pounds (140 kilograms). He traveled everywhere by train but was too big to get through the door of a passenger carriage so journeyed in the guard's van. He died in 1886 and his brother George managed the business until his son Gordon was 21. Gordon had been working as a distiller in South Africa.

Gordon died in 1912 and his widow Mary took over the day-to-day running of the distillery. World War I meant that the distillery had to close in 1917. Mary reopened Cragganmore in 1919 and installed electric light run by a petrol-driven generator. She sold the distillery in 1923 to Mackie & Co in 1923.

CRAGGANMORE CLASSIC MALTS SELECTION ™ 12 YEAR OLD 40% (80°)

Color   Light bronze.

Nose   This is a summer's day malt on the nose, bees buzzing over summer blossom, vanilla candy.

Taste   The mouth is completely different, the summer barbecue comes into play with light smoke and more complex caramel notes.

CRAGGANMORE DISTILLERS EDITION RUBY PORT WOOD FINISH 40% (80°)

Color   Light bronze with gold reflectance.

Nose   The port has added ripe summer fruits to the nose.

Taste   The fruits mix with the malts in a complex burst of flavor and then the smoke creeps through to give a dry, smoky finish with a hint of sweetness.

DALMORE

Highland

Dalmore Distillery
Alness, Ross-shire IV17 0UT
Tel: +44 1349 882362
www.thedalmore.com

OWNERS: WHYTE & MACKAY LIMITED

FOUNDED: 1839

VISITOR CENTER: YES

Dalmore is a half Gaelic, half ancient Norse name and means "the big meadowland" from the vast grassland of the Black Isle opposite the distillery. This is a beautiful part of Scotland with wooded hillsides and mudflats offering ornithologists a wealth of birds to see including waders and whooper swans.

Dalmore Distillery was built at Ardross Farm in 1839 by Alexander Matheson, a member of the Hong Kong trading company Jardine Matheson. The site was chosen because of its proximity to water and abundant supplies of local Easter Ross barley. Records show that from 1850 onward Margaret Sutherland was a "sometime distiller." By 1867 the distillery was in a bad state of repair and was purchased by Charles, Andrew, and Alexander Mackenzie. Alexander was interested in improving the distillery and by 1874 production had risen to 44,214 gallons (200,700 liters) from the first year's total of 16,380 gallons (74,360 liters). By this time they had started exporting Dalmore to Australia and New Zealand through Matheson & Co. The brothers purchased the distillery, adjoining farms, and pier in 1891.

During World War I Dalmore was forced to close. The Royal Navy used Dalmore to manufacture mines, so casks were moved for safety to neighboring warehouses. Distilling started again in 1920 and the family continued to run the company for three generations until 1960 when they merged with Whyte & Mackay Ltd.

Dalmore is available at 12, 21, and 30 years old and as The Dalmore Cigar Malt.

THE DALMORE 12 YEAR OLD 40% (80°)

Color Warm copper.

Nose Initial sulfur punch from Oloroso Sherry then crème brulée, smoke.

Taste Full bodied, caramel, warm fruit, licorice, and burned raisins.

THE DALMORE 21 YEAR OLD 43% (86°)

Color Deep copper with mahogany glow.

Nose Caramel, oranges, lemons, apples, marzipan, and vanilla.

Taste Warm fills the mouth with fruit, malt, and chocolate and honeyed bitter finish.

THE DALMORE CIGAR MALT 40% (80°)

Color Mahogany with copper flashes.

Nose Strong Sherry notes, burned crème caramel, nut crunch, cinnamon, and vanilla.

Taste Warm smooth wraps around the tongue filling with creamy toffee fudge, light licorice, and spice, a sweet finish with smoke.

DALWHINNIE

Highland

Dalwhinnie Distillery
Dalwhinnie, Inverness-shire PH19 1AB
Tel: +44 1540 672219
www.malts.com

OWNERS: DIAGEO

FOUNDED: 1897

VISITOR CENTER: YES

Dalwhinnie comes from the Gaelic for "the meeting place," a strategic crossing point for cattle drovers coming from the north and west. Here cattle rested for the climb over Drumtochter Pass toward the markets in the south. Dalwhinnie started as the Strathspey distillery and was built 1,073 feet (327 meters) above sea-level, close to the Lochan an Doire-uaine, which provided ample fresh water. Dalwhinnie is the second highest distillery in Scotland; Braeval is slightly higher.

The original owners were John Grant, a solicitor from Grantown-on-Spey, Alex Mackenzie, an architect from Kingussie, and George Sellar, a grocer from Kingussie, and distillation started in February 1898. The partnership was short-lived and the business went into liquidation. In October 1898 Strathspey was bought by a Mr. A. P. Blyth for his son. Charles Doig the distillery architect renovated the buildings and a siding was constructed to link with the main railroad track. The distillery was re-named Dalwhinnie.

In 1905 A. P. Blyth & Son sold to Cook & Bernheimer of New York, Baltimore, the biggest distillers in the United States. Cook & Bernheimer flew the American flag at their offices in Leith. Prohibition (1920-1933) cut short their involvement in Scotch whisky and in 1919 Dalwhinnie was sold to Macdonald Greenlees and Williams Ltd. In 1926 Distillers Company Limited bought the distillery.

Dalwhinnie is also one of the Meteorological Office's stations, and the manager takes daily readings of the prevailing weather conditions.

DALWHINNIE CLASSIC MALTS SELECTION ™
15 YEAR OLD 43% (86º)

Color   Summer gold.

Nose   Dry, complex summer aromas with light citrus.

Taste   A beautiful malt with the summer notes on the tongue, citrus and a lush, sweet finish with a hint of smoke. Dalwhinnie is one of the best introductory malts available.

DALWHINNIE DISTILLERS EDITION OLOROSO
FINISH 1985 43% (86º)

Color   Gold.

Nose   The Sherry finish makes a difference on the nose with sulfur, caramel notes, and smoke more pronounced.

Taste   In the mouth richer fruit and oak flavors.

EDRADOUR

Highland

Edradour Distillery
Pitlochry, Perthshire PH16 5JP
Tel: +44 1796 472095
www.edradour.com

OWNERS: SIGNATORY VINTAGE SCOTCH WHISKY CO LTD

FOUNDED: 1825

VISITOR CENTER: YES

Edradour has the distinction of being Scotland's smallest distillery. Whisky is distilled using the smallest stills permissible under UK Customs and Excise regulations.

Edradour started as a farm distillery at Glenforres on land rented from the Duke of Atholl. Today, it is not difficult to imagine yourself back there as the whitewashed distillery still resembles a collection of farm buildings. In 1841 the farmers created John MacGlashan & Co, which was purchased by J. G. Turney & Sons of the United States in 1886. In 1922 William Whiteley bought the distillery and started creating their own blends including King's Ransom and House of Lords. In 1975 the distillery became part of Pernod Ricard.

Edradour was purchased by Andrew Symington of Signatory in July 2002. At the time of the purchase he said, "To buy Edradour is a dream come true. Over the years I have looked at a number of distilleries as they came on to the market, but Edradour is a perfect complement to the Signatory business."

Edradour is available at 10 years old.

Additionally, Ballechin was released at the end of 2005. This is the first of a range of heavily peated malts (50ppm) matured in first fill Burgundy casks. Additional bottlings will come from a variety of casks including Oloroso Sherry, Port, Claret, Sauternes, and Madeira. Ballechin was one of seven farm distilleries along with Edradour operating in Perthshire, which closed in 1927.

EDRADOUR 10 YEAR OLD 40% (80°)

Color   Pale gold.

Nose   Delicate, sweet with a hint of peat.

Taste   Dry slightly sweet with a nutty smooth finish.

BALLECHIN BURGUNDY MATURED 46% (92°)

Color   Warm light copper gold.

Nose   Pungent with smoke, prunes, cherries, and oak.

Taste   There's a peat punch linked to rich fruit, caramel and spiced oak with a warm smoky finish. Satisfying, it is very difficult to believe that this is only four years old.

GLEN ELGIN

Speyside

Glen Elgin Distillery
Longmorn, Elgin, Morayshire IV30 3SL
Tel: +44 1343 862100
www.malts.com

OWNER: DIAGEO
FOUNDED: 1899
VISITOR CENTER: No

Glen Elgin was built from 1898–1900 and designed by Charles Doig. This was a time of whisky expansion, but the bubble burst when Pattisons of Leith, whisky blenders, were declared bankrupt. Glen Elgin was the last Speyside distillery to be built until 1957, when Glen Keith was constructed.

By 1901 the distillery was mothballed and up for sale. In 1907 Glen Elgin was bought by John J. Blanche, a whisky merchant from Glasgow. Glen Elgin only produced whisky for a short time during the next 23 years and changed hands several times. In 1930 it was purchased by Scottish Malt Distillers and the license transferred to White Horse Distillers. The distillery was powered by water until 1950 when electricity was introduced. Glen Elgin was rebuilt with new stills in 1992.

Glen Elgin is part of the Classic Malts Selection and special releases are available from time to time. The distillery continues to produce single malt for the White Horse Scotch Whisky and its light honey notes are a key component of this world-famous blend.

GLEN ELGIN 12 YEAR OLD 43% (86°)
CLASSIC MALTS SELECTION ™

Color   Gold.

Nose   Light smoke, honey, pear, and marzipan tart.

Taste   Medium-bodied malt with a slightly dry, peat taste, a hint of sweetness and a long finish. Glen Elgin has long been a favorite as an introductory malt.

GLEN GARIOCH

Highland

Glen Garioch Distillery
Old Meldrum, Inverurie, Aberdeenshire AB51 0ES
Tel: +44 1651 873450
www.glengarioch.com

OWNERS: MORRISON BOWMORE

FOUNDED: 1798

VISITOR CENTER: YES

Glen Garioch was founded by Thomas Simpson in 1798, although it is believed that he was producing spirit in 1785 on the same site. The distillery is in a fertile stretch of Aberdeenshire and there would have been a ready supply of local barley. The distillery was taken over by Ingram, Lamb & Co and there were several more owners until Stanley Morrison purchased Glen Garioch in 1970. The distillery had been taken out of production, so the new owner had to rebuild before distilling could start again.

Glen Garioch is bottled at 10, 15, and 21 years old with occasional special bottlings available from the distillery.

GLEN GARIOCH 10 YEAR OLD 40% (80°)

Color   Pale gold.

Nose   This is a light scented malt with hints of peat and orange blossom.

Taste   There are hints of fruit and honey, but on the whole a dry, malt taste with a medium finish.

GLEN GARIOCH 15 YEAR OLD 43% (86°)

Color   Gold.

Nose   Warmer, fruitier aroma with hints of oak.

Taste   A warm glowing whisky with citrus and smoke and a long mellow finish.

GLEN GRANT

Speyside

Glen Grant Distillery
Rothes, Morayshire AB38 7BS
Tel: +44 1340 832118
www.glengrant.com

OWNERS: DAVIDE CAMPARI – MILANO S.P.A.

FOUNDED: 1840

VISITOR CENTER: YES

There are distilleries with gardens, but to my knowledge only one garden with a distillery. Glen Grant sits in a secluded woodland garden with orchards, ponds, a cascading waterfall, and a safe built in the rock of the gorge.

Glen Grant was founded by John and James Grant in 1840. The Grants had previously leased Aberlour in 1833 together with the Walker brothers from Elgin. The site they chose was close to the Black Burn in a sheltered valley, with pure spring water from the Caperdonich Well on the hillside above. John died in 1864 and his brother James carried on running the distillery until his son James junior (known as the Major) joined in 1869 at the age of 22. He was to make Glen Grant a key player in the malt whisky market.

He was fascinated by innovations and Glen Grant was the first distillery to have electricity. He designed the tall stills with their unique purifiers to create his signature single malt. In 1897 he built Caperdonich distillery across the road, known as Glen Grant 2. The distillery was mothballed in 1902 and did not reopen until 1965. (Caperdonich now belongs to Chivas Brothers/Pernod Ricard.)

He also found time to create his Victorian garden which climbed up the hill toward the waterfall. The Major died in 1931 and the distillery was taken over by his grandson Douglas Mackessack. In 1961 Douglas Mackessack met Armando Giovinetti and Glen Grant became the most popular malt whisky in Italy. In 2006, most appropriately, the Campari Group acquired Glen Grant.

GLEN GRANT – AVAILABLE UNAGED 40% (80°),
5 YEAR OLD, 40% (80°), AND 10 YEAR OLD
40% (80°)
(I haven't tasted Glen Grant recently, so the following tasting notes are from Campari International Magazine, *Issue 17)*

"The whisky's fine aroma calls to mind citrus, flowers, pear, apple, vanilla, malt and wood, whilst its clean flavour is reminiscent of fruit, oranges, vanilla, liquorice and nuts."

GLEN MORAY

Speyside

Glen Moray Distillery
Elgin, Morayshire IV30 1YE
Tel: +44 1343 542577
www.glenmoray.com

OWNERS: THE GLENMORANGIE CO (MOËT HENNESSY)

FOUNDED: 1897

VISITOR CENTER: YES

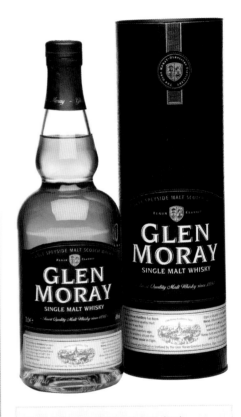

The distillery is on the banks of the River Lossie close to Gallow Hill, a site used for executions until the end of the 1600s. Glen Moray started life as a brewery in 1828 and whisky production started in 1897. The distillery closed in 1910 and in 1920 the owners sold the distillery to Macdonald & Muir, Leith-based whisky blenders and wine and spirit merchants who already owned Glenmorangie. There is a sense of timelessness at Glen Moray as the buildings still resemble an old Highland farm built around a courtyard.

In 1999 the company introduced finished versions of Glen Moray using Chardonnay and Chenin Blanc wine casks. Glen Moray along with other distilleries belonging to the Glenmorangie Co was purchased by Moët Hennessy in 2004.

Glen Moray is available at 8, 12, and 16 years old and also as Glen Moray Classic with Special Bottlings released from time to time.

GLEN MORAY 12 YEAR OLD 40% (80°)

Color   Summer gold.

Nose   Delicate, hints of summer with malt and dried fruits.

Taste   A medium-bodied malt with plenty of sweet toffee, malt, and dried fruit flavors and a medium warm slightly sweet finish.

GLEN MORAY CLASSIC 40% (80°)

Color   Pale summer sunshine.

Nose   Malt, fresh grass, and citrus and a hint of honey.

Taste   The light summer notes on the nose are replicated in the tongue with a dry, spicy finish.

GLEN ORD

Highland

Glen Ord Distillery
Muir of Ord, Ross-shire IV6 7UJ
Tel: +44 1463 872004
www.malts.com

**THE SINGLETON OF GLEN ORD CLASSIC MALTS
SELECTION 12 YEAR OLD 40% (80°)**

Color   Warm gold.

Nose   Full hints of caramel and spice and
        a subtle smoke backnote.

Taste   Smooth wrapping around the tongue,
        with malt summer fruit, and a dry
        honeyed finish.

OWNERS: DIAGEO

FOUNDED: 1838

VISITOR CENTER: YES

Glen Ord was founded in 1838 by Thomas Mackenzie in the heart of classic distilling country. *The New Statistical Account of Scotland* (1840) stated that "distilling aquavitae" was the main manufacturing activity in the area. There were nine other small distilleries and all the local barley was used to make whisky. Water for Glen Ord comes from Loch nan Eun and Loch nam Bonnach which flow into streams to the Allt Fionnaidh, "The White Burn."

Mackenzie licensed the distillery to Robert Johnstone and Donald MacLennan. In 1847 Robert Johnstone, who had become the sole licensee of the distillery, went bankrupt and it was purchased by Alexander MacLennan who was also declared insolvent. The distillery was inherited by his widow, who married Alexander McKenzie of Beauly, a banking agent. Mackenzie was a shrewd businessman and rebuilt the distillery after a fire in 1878 and registered the trademark in 1882.

When Alfred Barnard, author of *The Whisky Distilleries of the United Kingdom, 1887*, visited Glen Ord, the distillery was producing 80,000 gallons (363,200 liters), some of which was exported to "Singapore, South Africa and other colonies." The whisky was also sold in bottles under the brand name of Glen Oran.

In 1896 the distillery was sold to James Watson & Co. Ltd, whisky blenders of Dundee. It was acquired by Scottish Malt Distillers in 1930.

Glen Ord is one of only four distilleries to produce its own maltings. The Saladin and drum maltings at Glen Ord also fulfil the needs of six other distilleries.

GLENCADAM

Highland

Glencadam Distillery
Brechin, Angus DD9 7PA
Tel: +44 1356 622217
www.glencadam.com

OWNERS: ANGUS DUNDEE DISTILLERS

FOUNDED: 1825

VISITOR CENTER: No

Glencadam was licensed by George Cooper in 1825, although it is clear that the distillery was producing whisky far earlier. *A History of Brechin* dated 1818, says, "There is one extensive distillery in the town called the North Port . . . There is another neat Distillery, called the Glencadam Distillery. These distilleries supply a far purer spirit than was formerly drunk, under the name of smuggled whisky." In 1838 another article confirmed there were still 2 distilleries, 2 breweries, and 47 licensed premises. North Port, also known as Brechin distillery, was founded in 1820 and closed in 1983. Water for the distillery comes from Loch Lee.

David Scott started running Glencadam in 1827 and purchased the distillery from George Cooper in 1837. In 1852 Alexander Thompson took over Glencadam and in 1891 Gilmour Thomson & Co bought the distillery to ensure they had a supply of single malt for their blends. Gilmour Thomson's Royal Blend Scots Whisky was a favorite with the then HRH Prince of Wales and the label showed the Royal coat of arms and a stag.

In 1954 Hiram Walker purchased the distillery and modernized the distillery in 1959. Following various takeovers, the company became part of Allied Domecq's portfolio. Allied mothballed the distillery in 2000 and in 2003 Glencadam was given a new lease of life by Angus Dundee.

GLENCADAM 15 YEAR OLD 40% (80°)

Color   Light copper.

Nose   A soft summer breeze, light pear drops, green oak, grassy.

Taste   Very light smooth, honey, floral notes, reminds me of beachside honeycomb sweet, finish is a quick hello and then gently fades.

GLENDRONACH

Speyside/Highland

Glendronach Distillery
Forgue, Huntly, Aberdeenshire AN54 6DA
Tel: +44 1466 730202

OWNERS: CHIVAS BROTHERS PERNOD RICARD

FOUNDED: 1826

VISITOR CENTER: YES

The Glendronach was an early farm distillery and distilling started well before it was legalized. James Allardes, the owner of Glendronach, was one of the earliest to take out a license in 1826.

Glendronach's remote location meant that distilling could be carried on illegally for many years without interruption. On arrival at the distillery you will notice huge rook nests in the trees at the end of the drive. It is rumored that these birds alerted the workmen to the arrival of visitors, such as the exciseman. The Glendronach is still in an isolated rural setting and the distillery is fed by the Dronac Burn with Highland cattle in the fields next to the main house, which has its own walled garden.

Glendronach's position puts it on the edge of the Speyside region, so some books show this as a Highland single malt.

When carrying out some research for the previous owners, Allied Distillers, I found an article suggesting that the whisky was marketed as "Cobbie's Guid Glendronach" because James rented a local house Cobairdy for his lifetime. After a very bad start he succeeded in selling Glendronach in Edinburgh with the unwitting assistance of a couple of young ladies of dubious reputation. He had given them some of his whisky after another failed sales call and they became his word-of-mouth salesmen. Glendronach was soon seen in every bar and merchant in the city. I for one am very glad he didn't give up, as I enjoy a glass of Glendronach.

The Glendronach is matured in a mixture of ex-Bourbon barrels and Sherry butts.

THE GLENDRONACH 12 YEAR OLD 40% (80°)

Color	Light copper gold.
Nose	The sulfur notes of the Sherry are prevalent at first then the nose opens up to rich fruit cake and tobacco.
Taste	Medium bodied, fills the mouth with honey sweetness with smoky overtones and a dry, slightly sharp finish.

GLENFARCLAS

Speyside

Glenfarclas Distillery
Ballindalloch, Banffshire AB37 9BD
Tel: +44 1807 500209
www.glenfarclas.co.uk

OWNERS: J & G GRANT

FOUNDED: 1836

VISITOR CENTER: YES

In today's corporate world it is heart-warming to discover a family-owned business. There have been Grants at Glenfarclas since 1865 and today John Grant is firmly in charge with his son George making an important contribution to the company.

A distillery probably stood on the same site at Rechlerich farm since 1797, but it wasn't until 1836 that Robert Hay took out a license to distil. Glenfarclas means "glen of the green grassland" and it became a favorite stop for drovers on their way to market. Robert Hay died in 1865 and John Grant and his son George bought the distillery and leased it to John Smith of The Glenlivet. John Smith left in 1870 to set up Cragganmore and J & G Grant resumed management. In 1890 George Grant died and his widow Barbara ran the distillery until her sons John and George took over in 1895.

The distillery was rebuilt in 1896 and from then on the Grant family developed Glenfarclas and farming took second place.

In 1973 a visitor center was opened and tours end in a room fitted with the original oak panelling from the First Class Smoking Lounge and bar from an old passenger liner, the SS Empress of Australia. The Canadian Pacific passenger liner was dismantled at Rosyth shipyard in Scotland.

There are some single malts, which stand out from the crowd, and to my mind Glenfarclas is one of them.

GLENFARCLAS 10 YEAR OLD 40% (80°)

Color   Bright light gold.

Nose   Raisin Sherry notes with light spice and smoke.

Taste   Light honeyed smoothness with spice and raisins with a long, smooth finish.

GLENFARCLAS 15 YEAR OLD 46% (92°)

Color   Warm copper gold.

Nose   Sherry sulfur prickle at first then malted barley and intense caramel, orange, and vanilla.

Taste   Immensely satisfying, fills the mouth with caramel, candied citrus peel, cherries, oak and a warm finish with hints of licorice and vanilla. This continues to be my favorite Glenfarclas expression.

GLENFIDDICH

Speyside

Glenfiddich Distillery
Dufftown, Keith, Banffshire AB55 4DH
Tel: +44 1340 820373
www.glenfiddich.com

OWNERS: WILLIAM GRANT & SONS
FOUNDED: 1886
VISITOR CENTER: YES

William Grant was born on December 19, 1839 in Dufftown. William started working at the age of seven as a herdsman and his schooling was confined to the winter months, but he seems to have been a dutiful scholar. He was apprenticed to a shoemaker and in 1863 started working as a clerk at the Tininver lime works at Craichie. By then he was 24 and married with 3 children. After three years at the lime works, William became a bookkeeper at Mortlach distillery. He was promoted to manager after several years.

He dreamed of building his own distillery to create the "best dram in the valley." He eventually found a site in the Fiddich valley, close to the Robbie Dhu Springs. Together with his wife, two daughters, and six of his seven sons (the seventh was a schoolmaster who continued to work and provide an income for the family) he started building the distillery in 1886. Equipment was purchased from Mrs. Cummings at Cardhu (Cardow) Distillery. The first spirit flowed from the stills on Christmas Day 1887.

Glenfiddich is the only Highland Scotch whisky to be distilled, matured, and bottled at its own distillery.

William Grant & Son made the decision to start marketing Glenfiddich in 1963 and this opened up the current worldwide interest in malt whiskies. They were also one of the first companies to create a visitor center at the distillery.

GLENFIDDICH SPECIAL RESERVE 12 YEAR OLD
40% (80°)

Color   Pale gold.

Nose   A delicate fresh aroma with a hint of peat.

Taste   At first light, slightly dry then a fuller flavor develops with subtle, sweet overtones.

GLENFIDDICH SOLERA RESERVE 15 YEAR OLD
43% (86°)

Color   Medium gold.

Nose   Sherry notes sulfur. With a drop of water opens out to include caramel, light oak, raisins, and smoke.

Taste   Reminiscent of warm Christmas (dark fruit) pudding with vanilla oak notes, hazelnuts, and caramel sauce.

GLENGOYNE

Highland

Glengoyne Distillery
Dumgoyne, Nr Killearn, Glasgow G63 9LB
Tel: +44 1360 550254
www.glengoyne.com

OWNERS: IAN MACLEOD DISTILLERS

FOUNDED: 1833

VISITOR CENTER: YES

Glengoyne began in 1833 as Burnfoot Distillery on land owned by the Edmonstone family. George Connell took a lease and built the distillery and a warehouse, which is still in use today. In 1851 John MacLelland took over until 1867 when Archibald McLelland ran Burnfoot. He sold the distillery to Lang Brothers in 1876 who renamed it Glen Guin "Glen of the Wild Geese." In 1905 the name changed again to Glengoyne.

Glengoyne was bought by the Edrington Group in the 1960s and then in 2003 Ian Macleod Distillers Limited purchased the distillery.

Glengoyne is one of the few distilleries to use no peat when drying its barley. Glengoyne is available at 10, 12, 17, and 21 years old.

The visitor center is offering a unique experience at the time of writing this book (February 2007). The Master Blending Course offers guests the chance to try a selection of Glengoyne whiskies and create their own blend — call the visitor center or visit the website to find out more.

GLENGOYNE 10 YEAR OLD 40% (80°)

Color   Pale lemon gold.

Nose   Light, lemon and honey.

Taste   Smooth, creamy subtle sweetness with a long, dry recurring finish.

GLENGOYNE 17 YEAR OLD 43% (86°)

Color   Pale burnished gold.

Nose   Subtle, warm scented notes, vanilla, honey, hints of apple and apricot.

Taste   Light, creamy, sweet with orange, deliciously smooth, malty, orchard fruits, and a hint of pepper spice, a long finish and a fine whisky.

GLENKINCHIE

Lowland

Glenkinchie Distillery
Pentcaitland, East Lothian EH34 5ET
Tel: +44 1875 342004
www.malts.com

OWNERS: DIAGEO

FOUNDED: 1837

VISITOR CENTER: YES

John and George Rate founded the distillery in 1837, having previously run the Milton distillery on the same site from 1825 to 1833. In 1853 production stopped and the distillery sold to a local farmer who turned it into a sawmill. In 1880 the distillery was restarted by a group of local Edinburgh businessmen and the Glenkinchie Distillery Company was founded 10 years later. In 1914 Glenkinchie, with four other Lowland distilleries, Rosebank, Clydesdale, St. Magdalene, and Grange, formed Scottish Malt Distilleries (SMD). Today, Glenkinchie is the only one of these Lowland distilleries still in production. In 1925 the Distillers Company Limited purchased SMD. It is interesting to note that in 1837, when Glenkinchie was built, there were 115 licensed distilleries operating in the Lowlands.

During World War II Glenkinchie was one of the very few distilleries allowed to produce small quantities of whisky each year. The majority were closed down as the Government restricted the amount of barley to be used for distilling.

Glenkinchie stopped malting its own barley in 1968. At the same time equipment was being thrown out by other distilleries in the group. It was decided to preserve much of this material and to create the Museum of Malt Whisky Production inside the old maltings facilities. This includes a model of a Highland malt whisky distillery, which was built for the British Empire Exhibition in 1924. Glenkinchie is close to Edinburgh and its visitor center welcomes more than 40,000 tourists each year.

GLENKINCHIE CLASSIC MALTS SELECTION ™
10 YEAR OLD 43% (86°)

Color   Pale gold.

Nose   Orange blossom and honey, hay, and malt.

Taste   A smooth light malt with a rounded flavor a hint of sweetness and smoke and a long finish.

GLENKINCHIE DISTILLERS EDITION
AMONTILLADO FINISH 1988 43% (86°)

Color   Warm gold.

Nose   Sweet vanilla and dry nutty notes open up to light fruit and malted barley.

Taste   Medium-bodied dry single malt with barley, fruits, and hints of caramel with a long dry finish.

THE GLENLIVET

Speyside

The Glenlivet Distillery
Ballindalloch, Banffshire AB37 9DB
Tel: +44 1340 821270
www.theglenlivet.com

OWNERS: CHIVAS BROTHERS PERNOD RICARD

FOUNDED: 1824

VISITOR CENTER: YES

Tales of pistols, illegal distillers, excisemen, and smugglers are all part of the history of Scotch whisky and in particular, The Glenlivet distillery founded by George Smith.

George's father, Andrew, started distilling at Upper Drumin in 1784. George started working as a laborer for his uncle and rented a small farm from him. By 1922 whisky from the Glenlivet area had become famous for its fine quality and on a visit to Edinburgh, King George IV asked for a glass of The Glenlivet by name.

In 1823 an Act of Parliament set a foundation for the fair taxation of spirits so that distillers could earn a living. George was the first distiller to take out a license. His neighbors were horrified and saw their livelihood threatened by his actions. They terrorized him and his family and tried to burn down the distillery. George kept a pair of hair-trigger pistols continually by his side and managed to prevent anything happening. These pistols are today on display in the Glenlivet visitor center.

George expanded his farm by leasing Castleton in 1838, Nevie in 1839, and Minmore in 1840 and leased Cairngorm distillery. In 1845 George took over the lease of Minmore on the banks of the River Livet. By 1862 George owned 600 acres and had 15 men working for him.

The distillery stayed in the Smith family until 1970. The Glenlivet was the first Scotch single malt whisky to be seen in the United States after Prohibition (1920–33).

THE GLENLIVET 12 YEAR OLD 40% (80°)

Color   Pale gold.

Nose   A light, fragrant malt with pineapple, fresh summer blossom.

Taste   Medium-bodied with tropical fruits and vanilla, which is not evident initially on the nose. A soft fading finish.

THE GLENLIVET 18 YEAR OLD 43% (86°)

Color   Warm copper gold with red highlights.

Nose   Malt is first element, raising fruitiness and dark chocolate, vanilla honey follows.

Taste   Smooth velvety, honeyed ginger fudge, oranges fading into a dry, light spice, short finish. There is a Sherry cask influence here.

GLENMORANGIE

Highland

Glenmorangie Distillery
Tain, Ross-shire IV19 1PZ
Tel: +44 1862 892043
www.glenmorangie.com

OWNERS: THE GLENMORANGIE CO (MOËT HENNESSY)

FOUNDED: 1843

VISITOR CENTER: YES

Glenmorangie ("the glen of tranquillity") is a distillery with a difference. The story began in 1738 when brewing started on Morangie Farm using water from the Tarlogie Spring. William Mathieson obtained the first license to distil whisky in Tain in 1843. In spite of limited equipment he produced 20,000 gallons of whisky annually. In 1887 the Glenmorangie Distillery Company Ltd was formed and complete rebuilding took place including new stills. These are unique; at 16 feet 10 inches high (5.13 meters) they are the tallest pot stills in Scotland.

In 1880 Glenmorangie started selling overseas to markets as diverse as Rome and San Francisco. In 1920 the distillery was purchased by Macdonald and Muir. Based in Leith, Macdonald and Muir were well-known distillers, blenders, and wine and spirit merchants. They sold Glenmorangie as a single malt in the 1920s, albeit in small quantities.

In 1996 Glenmorangie launched a range of finished whiskies, which commemorate the fact that Macdonald and Muir traded in fine wines and spirits. Their first finished whisky, an 18 year old with a percentage re-racked in Sherry casks, was in fact released in 1992, although the label didn't show this. The first labeled bottlings were Glenmorangie Sherry Wood Finish, Glenmorangie Madeira Finish, and Glenmorangie Port Wood Finish. In November 2007 Glenmorangie was rebranded with new expressions Lasanta, Quinta Ruban, and Nectar D'or.

GLENMORANGIE ORIGINAL 40% (80º)

Color   Pale straw-summer.

Nose   Minty fresh, cut grass, floral, vanilla, black currant leaves.

Taste   Light, soft hints of blackcurrant, flowers, and vanilla with a short finish.

GLENMORANGIE NECTAR D'OR
UNCHILLFILTERED 46% (92º)

Color   Warm honey gold.

Nose   Almond pastry, lemon meringue pie, and baked pears.

Taste   A smooth mellow dram with caramel and cream, hints of lemon, and warm spice.

GLENROTHES

Speyside

Glenrothes Distillery
Rothes, Morayshire AB38 7AA
Tel: +44 1340 872300
www.theglenrothes.com

OWNERS: THE EDRINGTON GROUP

FOUNDED: 1878

VISITOR CENTER: No

The Glenrothes was started by Robert Dick and William Grant from the Caledonian Bank, and John Cruickshank, a lawyer, in 1878 and production started on December 28, 1879. Glenrothes distillery's water supply comes from The Lady's Well. Apparently this was where the only daughter of a fourteenth century Earl of Rothes was murdered by the "Wolf of Babenoch" while trying to save her lover's life.

In 1887 the Glenrothes Distillery and the Islay Distillery Company, owner of Bunnahabhain Distillery got together to form Highland Distillers. In 1922 after a fire in the warehouse, whisky poured into the Burn of Rothes. The story is that the local population and indeed a few cows took advantage of this free drink.

From the beginning, Glenrothes was highly prized by blenders including Cutty Sark and The Famous Grouse. One of the key companies to use Glenrothes was the London-based wine and spirit merchants Berry Bros & Rudd Ltd, which was founded in 1698. The Glenrothes is marketed by Berry, Bros & Rudd, who decided to declare vintages in much the same way as wines are sold. Casks are chosen from a specific year representing the Glenrothes character but with a slightly different personality. This is different from the concept of creating aged expressions, which are always similar.

The Glenrothes Vintages I have tasted include 1975, 1985, 1994, and 1991, and the Select Reserve. I think the Glenrothes should be classified as a happy malt, it lifts the heart and tongue; a malt you want to hug.

GLENROTHES 1975 43% (86°)

Color   Warm honey gold.

Nose   Orange with vanilla, honey, and creamy fudge.

Taste   Warm citrus flavors mingle with creamy fudge, hints of cinnamon and smooth, lingering finish. A superb after-dinner drink.

GLENROTHES 1991 DISTILLED 7TH SEPTEMBER 1991 BOTTLED 24TH MAY 2005 43% (86°)

Color   Warm golden bronze.

Nose   Honey, orange blossoms, raspberries, and vanilla.

Taste   Mature, smooth, classy malt, butterscotch, honeyed sweetness with candied orange, cloves, and a coconut ice-cream finish.

HIGHLAND PARK

Orkney/Highland

Highland Park Distillery
Holm Road, Kirkwall, Orkney KW15 1SU
Tel: +44 1856 874619
www.highlandpark.co.uk

OWNERS: EDRINGTON GROUP

FOUNDED: 1798

VISITOR CENTER: YES

Highland Park is the northernmost distillery in Scotland on the mainland of the Orkney Isles. This is one of my favorite distilleries – I remember well my first visit with my business colleague Patrick Gallagher and Matthew Gloag from The Famous Grouse dynasty. We sat on the beach on a bright February day with the sun shining on the water and the ruins of Skara Brae, an ancient burial site, behind us.

Illicit stills were quite common on Orkney when David Robertson founded Highland Park in 1798. The site was chosen because the springs from Cattie Maggie's pool provided crystal-clear water. Highland Park still malts 20 percent of its own grain requirement on traditional floor maltings and most of the barley is grown locally. The malt is lightly peated using peat dug from distillery fields.

In 1826 Highland Park was bought by Robert Borwick and from then on the history is well documented. The distillery was purchased by Highland Distilleries, now part of the Edrington Group, in 1935.

The distillery visitor center at Highland Park gives an insight to the production of this very special single malt and the beautiful Orkney Isles – don't miss it!

Highland Park is available at 12, 15, 18, 25, and 30 years old. Highland Park Single Cask and other special editions are released from time to time. I only have to drink Highland Park and I am back on Orkney with the sea in front of me and the heather behind and it is unquestionably a favorite of mine.

HIGHLAND PARK 12 YEAR OLD 40% (80°)

Color   Deep gold like sunset over Scapa Flow.

Nose   Rich, smoky, with a hint of honey.

Taste   A gloriously rounded malt with heather, peat, and warm nutty overtones. Fills the mouth and the flavors just keep on coming. A dry finish with a hint of sweetness.

HIGHLAND PARK 25 YEAR OLD 50.7% (101.4°)

Color   Amber copper streaked gold.

Nose   Hot summer day on the Orkneys! Warm honey heather, vanilla, summer blossoms.

Taste   Warm, sunshine on the beach, toffee, orange marmalade, smoke, fresh ginger, and spice. Smoke and honey lingering finish.

JURA

Isle of Jura/Highland

Isle of Jura Distillery
Craighouse, Jura, Argyllshire PA60 7XT
Tel: +44 1496 820385
www.isleofjura.com

OWNERS: WHYTE AND MACKAY LIMITED

FOUNDED: 1810

VISITOR CENTER: YES

If you want to get away from it all then Jura is the place. The Isle of Jura is home to more wild deer than human inhabitants and was used as a getaway by the writer George Orwell. The distillery sits on the edge of the seashore with the Paps of Jura climbing behind it and palm trees in the garden.

Jura was founded in 1810 by Archibald Campbell as the Small Isles Distillery. The distillery was licensed in 1831 and renamed the Isle of Jura Distillery. There were many changes of ownership during the next 70 years and in 1901 the distillery closed because the licensee at the time, James Ferguson, was in dispute with the landowner Colin Campbell. In 1920 Campbell took the roof off the distillery so that he could stop paying tax. It wasn't until 1960 that Charles Mackinlay & Co rebuilt the distillery, and by the time the first new spirit ran from the stills in 1963 the new owners were Scottish & Newcastle.

Today, the distillery is part of the Whyte and Mackay portfolio. Jura is available in a range of expressions including Superstition, a mix of peated young and older malts (all of course distilled at Jura), and Jura 10 year old, 16 year old, and 21 year old. Seven years ago, Richard Paterson, the company's Master Blender, started looking at the wood policy to ensure that casks are selected so that the essential elements of each single malt are reflected in the final bottlings. The latest bottlings of Jura reflect this attention to detail and to my mind offer whisky drinkers just that little bit extra.

JURA 10 YEAR OLD 40% (80°)

Color   Warm amber.

Nose   Peat smoke, spirity, malt nose.
        With a little water this expands
        to Sherry sweetness.

Taste   In the mouth light honey and smoke
        combine, light creamy mouthfeel,
        hints of coffee and a long dry finish.

JURA SUPERSTITION 45% (90°)

Color   Warm copper gold.

Nose   Rich and welcoming, wood fires, fruit
        cake, and malt.

Taste   Burned caramel, prunes, warm, satisfying
        with a hint of smoke and long, rich finish
        making this a very good dram.

KILCHOMAN

Islay

Kilchoman Distillery
Rockside Farm, Bruichladdich, Isle of Islay PA49 7UT
Tel: +44 1496 850011
www.kilchomandistillery.com

OWNERS: ANTHONY WILLS

FOUNDED: 2001

VISITOR CENTER: YES

Kilchoman is an exciting development on an island known for its individuality. The increased interest in Islay single malt whiskies prompted Anthony Willis and other investors to start a farm distillery on Islay in 2001. The last distillery to be built on Islay was Bruichladdich in 1881.

If you have visited Islay you will know Kilchoman for its fifteenth-century Celtic cross and the wide sweep of Machir Bay. You may well have eaten prime beef from Rockside Farm owned by Mark French. Mark and Anthony have been friends for a long time and it seemed only natural that the new distillery should be located in old buildings at Rockside. Anthony Willis also runs Liquid Gold Enterprises, a specialty bottling company marketing Caledonian Selection, Spirit of the Isles, and Celtic Legends ranges.

The passage from old farm building to micro-distillery has been a slow, hard one with problems, such as a fire, along the way. However, anyone visiting Kilchoman will find a model distillery and a superb visitor center and café. The distillery was officially opened on Friday June 3, 2005, during the Islay Whisky Festival.

Kilchoman reflects the early traditional farm distilleries using barley grown on the farm and malted on a malt floor at the distillery. Everything is on-site from barley to the spirit in a bottle.

New spirit is available from the distillery, and the first whisky bottling will take place in 2010, when the spirit will be four years old.

KILCHOMAN NEW SPIRIT DISTILLATION DATE 29TH MAY 2006 PHENOL LEVEL 35PPMILLION 69% (138°)

Color   Clear spirit as you would expect.

Nose   Peat smoke, malt and leather and surprisingly smooth with no spirit prickle.

Taste   The peat smoke fills the mouth, creamy mouthfeel, hint of sweetness – this promises to be a very good whisky, I for one cannot wait till 2010 to try it at four years' old.

KNOCKANDO

Speyside

Knockando Distillery
Knockando, Morayshire AB38 7RT
Tel: +44 1340 882001
www.malts.com

OWNERS: DIAGEO

FOUNDED: 1898

VISITOR CENTER: NO

Knockando is Gaelic for "little black hill." The distillery was built for John Thomson in 1898 of the Knockando-Glenlivet Distillery Co on the banks of the River Spey. Water for Knockando is taken from the Cardnach spring. Knockando was the first Speyside distillery to have electric lighting installed.

The distillery started production in 1899, but suffered because of the Pattison crash and the business was transferred to J. Thomson & Co in 1900. In 1904 W. A. Gilbey Ltd purchased the distillery and the following year Knockando was connected to the Great North of Scotland Railway to speed up delivery throughout Britain. W. A. Gilbey merged with United Wine Traders, which included Justerini & Brooks in 1962. In 1975, the group was taken over by Watney Mann and later that year became part of IDV Grand Metropolitan. The number of stills was increased, by the new owners, from two to four. Knockando has been the key signature malt in J & B Rare for quite some considerable time. Knockando was first exported in 1978 and is now available worldwide.

Knockando is a lightly peated malt, matured in refill Bourbon with a small percentage of Sherry casks to give color to the final whisky.

Knockando is now part of the extended Classic Malts range and is available at 12, 18, and 21 years old.

KNOCKANDO CLASSIC MALTS SELECTION ™
12 YEAR OLD 40% (80°)

Color   Pale lemon gold.

Nose   Warm, fragrant, spicy.

Taste   Warm caramel with spice, vanilla, and echoes of hazelnut and malt.

KNOCKDHU

Speyside

Knockdhu Distillery
Knock, By Huntly, Aberdeenshire AB5 5LI
Tel: +44 1466 771223
www.inverhouse.com

OWNERS: INVER HOUSE DISTILLERS
FOUNDED: 1893
VISITOR CENTER: No

Knockdhu was built by Distillers Company for Haig's. The distillery was built near springs containing pure, clear water, which run down from the southern slopes of Knockdhu — the Black Hill. The distillery started production in October 1894 and as many as 3,000 gallons (11,340 liters) were distilled each week from the two steam driven pot stills. Most of the distillery's production was destined for blended whisky.

The distillery closed in 1931, reopened in 1933, and then closed again in 1983. Inver House bought Knockdhu from United Distillers in 1988 and production restarted the following year. Inver House took the decision to launch a single malt as Knockdhu in 1990 but were under pressure to change the name because it might be confused with Knockando, another distillery owned by United Distillers. From 1993 all bottlings are labeled AnCnoc.

AnCnoc is currently available at 12 and 14 years with a few limited editions.

ANCNOC 12 YEAR OLD 40% (80°)

Color   Pale summer gold.

Nose   Malty dry with toasted hazelnuts and aniseed.

Taste   Light honeyed sweetness wrapping around bitter hazelnuts and a hint of aniseed, dry complex finish.

ANCNOC 1975 50% (100°)

Color   Pale summer gold.

Nose   Dried fruits, hint of caramel, and pear drops.

Taste   Dry maltiness expands to fill the mouth with hints of bitter orange, toffee, and spice with a long finish.

LAGAVULIN

Islay

Lagavulin Distillery
Port Ellen, Islay, Argyll PA42 7DZ
Tel: +44 1496 302400
www.malts.com

OWNERS: DIAGEO

FOUNDED: 1816

VISITOR CENTER: YES (BY APPOINTMENT)

Stories of deception and treachery are closely linked to the early days of whisky distilling in Scotland. The history of Lagavulin is a tale of stolen water, disputes, and intrigue.

The first thing visitors see as they approach to Lagavulin are the ruins of Dunyveg Castle, where the Lords of the Isles met and sent soldiers to wage war on the mainland.

Lagavulin started life as two distilleries. The first was built in 1816 by John Johnston and the second alongside in 1817 by Archibald Campbell. In 1837 both distilleries worked together producing Lagavulin. In 1852 and 1857 James Logan Mackie, uncle of Peter Mackie, the founder of White Horse, bought Lagavulin. Peter inherited the distillery in 1878.

This is where things started to get interesting. Peter Mackie was also agent for Laphroaig, the neighboring distillery. The owners of Laphroaig felt their sales were poor and terminated their contract with him in 1907. Mackie retaliated by cutting off the water supply. Laphroaig's owners took Mackie to court and he was ordered to restore water to the distillery. Mackie then set about building a distillery, which would exactly replicate Laphroaig inside Lagavulin, which he called Malt Mill. Despite his efforts he never produced a whisky exactly like Laphroaig.

All of this seems crazy today, when you consider that Lagavulin is one of the most sought after single malts in the world.

LAGAVULIN CLASSIC MALTS SELECTION ™ 16 YEAR OLD 43% (86°)

Color   Warm summer gold.

Nose   A very powerful peaty aroma.

Taste   Full bodied pungent peat flavor with undertones of sweetness and a long smoke and salt laden finish.

LAGAVULIN DISTILLERS EDITION PEDRO XIMENEZ FINISH 43% (86°)

Color   Golden bronze.

Nose   The Sherry gives a warm burst of caramel initially and then the nose expands to include sea spray, hot tarmac roads, and peat smoke.

Taste   The mouth is filled with burned caramel and then the sea salt and smoke invade wrapping themselves around the tongue to create a long dry finish.

LAPHROAIG

Islay

Laphroaig Distillery
Port Ellen, Isle of Islay PA42 7DU
Tel: +44 1496 302418
www.laphroaig.com

OWNERS: FORTUNE BRANDS

FOUNDED: 1810

VISITOR CENTER: YES

Laphroaig was founded by farmers Alexander and Donald Johnston and remained in the family until 1954 when Ian Hunter left the distillery to Bessie Williamson. Bessie came from Glasgow in the late 1930s to Laphroaig and became interested in whisky production. Bessie joined the peat cutters, learnt to nose and taste young whisky, and involved herself in all aspects of distillery and island life. When Ian Hunter had a stroke on a sales trip to America in 1938, Bessie went out and finished the sales tour for him. Ian never fully recovered from his stroke and at the end of World War II he appointed Bessie as his distillery manager.

The captains of the small steam "Puffers" who brought supplies to the distillery would probably recognize the distillery today, for much of it looks the same as it would have 100 years ago. The Puffers' journey would not have been an easy one and they had to negotiate the rocks which surround the Laphroaig bay. Once inside the bay the distillery workers would tie up the boats to big iron rings in the rocks in an effort to keep the boats steady.

Purchasers of a bottle of Laphroaig are given the opportunity to put their name on a square-foot of Islay. These small parcels of land are across the road from the distillery and from time to time you can see people wandering around in wellington boots trying to work out where their plot is.

Laphroaig is one of three distilleries on Islay to have its own maltings, which provides 20 percent of the total requirement.

LAPHROAIG 10 YEAR OLD CASK STRENGTH
57.7% (111.4°)

Color   Light gold.

Nose   Packs a punch, peat smoke, sea salt, Coal tar, hot sun on a tarmac road, with a hint of sweetness in the background.

Taste   The sweetness comes through first, then peat smoke and sea salt in waves, wrapping around the caramel and coating the mouth with smoke.

LAPHROAIG QUARTER CASK (NO AGE SHOWN)
48% (96°)

Color   Pale gold.

Nose   Sweet barley and peat.

Taste   In the mouth it's warm, luscious, and syrupy, there's a hint of peaches and creamed coconut, and then a real peat bang. As it slips down the sweetness in the mouth lingers with roasted peat barley – long lingering and scrumptious.

LONGMORN

Speyside

Longmorn Distillery
Nr Elgin, Morayshire IV30 3SJ
Tel: +44 1542 783400
www.chivas.com

OWNERS: CHIVAS BROTHERS PERNOD RICARD

FOUNDED: 1894

VISITOR CENTER: NO

Longmorn distillery is on the road to Rothes from Elgin. The name Longmorn comes from the small church of St. Marnoch or Maernanog. Saint Marnoch brought Christianity to the area in the seventh century.

Longmorn was built in 1893 by Charles Shirres, George Thomson, and John Duff on land leased at Longmorn Farm. The cost of building Longmorn amounted to £20,000. John Duff was already one of the Scotch whisky industry's leading businessmen and saw the potential for a new distillery. Power for the distillery was provided by a large water-wheel – this is still on site, but is no longer operational. The distillery began working in December 1894.

The site was chosen because there were ample supplies of peat and pure spring water from the Mannoch Hill. Longmorn was also close to the railroad which provided good links with the customers down south. Much of the Aberdeen to Elgin Railway and Keith & Dufftown Railway still exist and they link most of the Speyside distilleries, although today they carry more passengers than whisky.

Following the Pattison crash the company was taken over by Hill, Thomson & Co Ltd. Longmorn was purchased by its current owners Chivas Brothers in 1978.

Longmorn is a well respected single malt and has been a favorite with blenders for a long time.

LONGMORN 16 YEAR OLD 48% (96°)

Color — Summer coppery gold.

Nose — Light, warm summer fragrances with honeysuckle.

Taste — Rich honey with strawberries and cream, shortbread with spiced nutmeg. A medium finish with hints of heather, smoke, and caramel.

THE MACALLAN

Speyside

The Macallan Distillery
Craigellachie, Banffshire AB38 9RX
Tel: +44 1340 872280
www.themacallan.com

OWNERS: EDRINGTON GROUP

FOUNDED: 1824

VISITOR CENTER: YES

The Macallan was licensed by Alexander Reid in 1824, close to a ford across the River Spey at Easter Elchies. Easter Elchies Manor became part of the distillery. After several changes of ownership, Roderick Kemp bought the Macallan in 1892.

Through Roderick Kemp's efforts, The Macallan became a favorite with whisky blenders. In 1975 the number of stills increased to 21. In 1979 his descendant Allan Schiach of the United States took over and the distillery started maturing its whisky in Sherry casks. The company started buying its own casks from Jerez in Spain. The whisky was marketed as Macallan–Glenlivet until 1980. After Roderick's death in 1909 the distillery passed to a family trust until it became part of Highland Distilleries in 1996.

Today Macallan is one of the world's most highly prized single malts. Several whisky connoisseurs have created their own collections. Ulf Buxrud of Sweden was one of them. I say was, because on April 20, 2002 he invited friends to celebrate his 60th birthday at the Landmark hotel in London and share 53 different The Macallan single malts dating from 1942. I was lucky enough to be master of ceremonies at this very special event. What a generous man Ulf is!

Having built up a cult following with its trademark sherried The Macallan, the company launched The Macallan Fine Oak range in 2004. The Fine Oak expressions are created from a mix of Bourbon and Sherry casks.

THE MACALLAN 1952 50.8% (101.6º)

Color   Warm amber.

Nose   Fresh, clean, Sherry notes but no sulfur, burned caramel, and vanilla.

Taste   The freshness on the nose is replicated in the mouth with caramelized oranges, nut praline, a hint of smoke and licorice, and a sweet, warm yet dry finish.

THE MACALLAN SHERRY OAK 10 YEAR OLD 40% (80º)

Color   Pale summer gold.

Nose   Light, fragrant, honeyed Sherry notes.

Taste   Full-bodied Sherry with hints of vanilla and fruit a long smooth well-rounded finish.

OBAN

Highland

Oban Distillery
Stafford Street, Oban, Argyllshire PA34 5NH
Tel: +44 1631 572002
www.malts.com

OWNERS: DIAGEO

FOUNDED: 1794

VISITOR CENTER: YES

Oban was built in 1794 by the Stevenson family, who turned a small fishing village into a thriving town.

The distillery is built up against the cliffs overlooking the harbor and externally it has remained virtually unchanged for 100 years. Oban is the main port for Skye and many tourists take advantage of a short break in the town to stay in one of the comfortable older-style hotels on the seafront and visit the distillery.

Oban was visited by Professor Jeffray of Glasgow for the House of Commons Committee on Distilleries in Scotland in 1798 and he reported that, "At Oban I found things in a much better situation" than elsewhere in the Highlands, "the distillery had been fitted up for a brewery; the barns were large and the granary ample. The person who had the charge of the work had been bred a distiller in the Lowlands." In 1819 Hugh became Oban's provost and he transferred ownership of the distillery and his other business interests, which included farms, a partly built hotel, and the Island of Belnahua with its quarries, to his son, Thomas. (Provost is the Scottish word for a local magistrate.)

Thomas did not inherit the Stevenson family's business acumen and by 1829 he was declared bankrupt. In 1830, his son, John purchased the distillery from his father's trustees. By 1925 Oban became part of the Distillers Company.

OBAN CLASSIC MALTS SELECTION ™
14 YEAR OLD 43% (86°)

Color   Pale gold.

Nose   Dried lemon, orange, and passion fruit with a floor polish backnote.

Taste   Spice notes on the front of the tongue, honey and candied fruits, dryness on the back of the tongue, with a sweet edge, dry pepper finish.

OBAN DISTILLERS EDITION 1989 BOTTLED 2003
MONTILLA FINO 43% (86°)

Color   Light coppery gold.

Nose   Initially buttered popcorn, resin, oregano, and a hint of spice.

Taste   Full bodied with warm, honeyed notes. Light rich fruit cake with sea salt and malt. A sweet, medium finish. Do not add water to this in my opinion as the taste becomes a bit rubbery rather like old wellington boots and the sulfur Sherry notes take over.

PULTENEY

Highland

Pulteney Distillery
Huddart Street, Wick, Caithness KW1 5BA
Tel: +44 1955 602371
www.oldpulteney.com

OWNERS: INVER HOUSE DISTILLERS

FOUNDED: 1826

VISITOR CENTER: YES

Pulteney is one of only two distilleries named after a person, the other is Glen Grant. Sir William Pulteney was Chairman of the British Fisheries Society and was responsible for the new fishing harbor and housing area, known as Pulteneytown, built on the other side of the river from the town of Wick. Pulteney is the most northerly mainland distillery.

Pulteney was founded in 1826 by James Henderson who had previously run his own distillery for 30 years. He decided to build a new distillery near the coast at Wick, which was a thriving herring fishing port. The locals unfortunately gained a reputation for drunkenness, and as a result local Prohibition was introduced and Wick became a dry town. The distillery continued to distil whisky throughout this time. Prohibition was lifted in 1947.

In 1920 the distillery was purchased by James Watson and in 1923 the Buchanan-Dewar group acquired Pulteney. The distillery closed in 1930 and reopened again in 1951 when bought by Robert Cumming who also owned Balblair. In 1955 the distillery was acquired by Hiram Walker (later Allied Distillers) and rebuilt in 1958. Inver House purchased the distillery from Allied Distillers in 1995.

Pulteney is bottled as Old Pulteney at 12, 17, and 21 years old with occasional special releases. The labels depict a picture of a traditional Wick herring drifter.

OLD PULTENEY 12 YEAR OLD 40% (80°)

Color Deep amber with flashes of copper.

Nose A dry, salty, slightly sweet aroma.

Taste The proximity of the distillery to the sea is palpable in the initial salty taste, but this is quickly replaced by hints of peat, allspice, and soft caramel. A short, crisp finish.

OLD PULTENEY 17 YEAR OLD 46% (92°)

Color Amber gold.

Nose Honeyed lemon blossom and citrus, fresh summer, and malt.

Taste The citrus notes on the notes are replicated in the mouth with malted barley and a hint of salt. A sumptuous malt with a warm, spiced, caramel finish.

ROYAL LOCHNAGAR

Highland

Royal Lochnagar Distillery
Crathie, Ballater, Aberdeenshire AB35 5TB
Tel: +44 1339 742700
www.malts.com

OWNERS: DIAGEO

FOUNDED: 1845

VISITOR CENTER: YES

There were a couple of attempts to build distilleries on the River Dee, but they were both burned down. James Robertson of Crathie took out a license in 1826, and it is believed that unlicensed distillers were responsible for the fire. *The Aberdeen Journal* wrote on May 12, 1841, "Fire at Lochnagar Distillery — On Thursday morning last, at four o'clock, the premises were discovered to be on fire; and notwithstanding the greatest exertions, the whole of the distillery house, malt barn, kiln, and store-rooms, with all their contents, were reduced to embers . . . "

Finally in 1845 John Begg built New Lochnagar on the south bank. Water for the distillery comes from springs in the foothills of Lochnagar Mountain. In 1848 John wrote to his new neighbor at Balmoral, Queen Victoria, as recorded in his diary: "I wrote a note on the 11th September to Mr G. E. Anson (Her Majesty's Private Secretary) stating that the distillery was now in full operation and would be so until six o'clock next day, and knowing how anxious HRH Prince Albert was to patronise and make himself acquainted with everything of a mechanical nature, I said I should feel much pleasure in showing him the works." The Royal family came the following day and after visiting the distillery they tasted some of the mature spirit. Clearly the visit was a success as within a very short time John Begg received the Royal Warrant.

The distillery remained in the Begg family until 1916 when Royal Lochnagar was sold to John Dewar & Sons.

ROYAL LOCHNAGAR CLASSIC MALTS SELECTION ™ 12 YEAR OLD 40% (80°)

Color   Pale summer gold.

Nose   Warm, spicy.

Taste   A whisky to savor with fruit, malt, and a hint of vanilla and oak, with a sweet long-lasting finish.

SCAPA

Orkney/Highland

Scapa Distillery
St Ola, Orkney KW15 1SE
Tel: +44 1856 872071
www.chivas.com

OWNERS: CHIVAS BROTHERS PERNOD RICARD

FOUNDED: 1885

VISITOR CENTER: No

Scapa is situated on the Orkney Islands and is therefore one of Scotland's most northerly distilleries. It is situated on the banks of the Lingro Burn and overlooks Scapa Flow. The Orkney Isles are very beautiful and visitors can be rewarded with superb walks, rock climbing, and bird watching.

The distillery was founded by Macfarlane and Townsend on the site of a former meal mill. Scapa has had a checkered career; the distillery ceased production in 1934, then started again in 1936 when the Bloch Brothers took it over to use in their blend Ambassador. In 1954 Hiram Walker took over and the distillery was rebuilt in 1959, but closed again in 1994. The future seemed uncertain, but in 2004 then owners Allied Distillers started rebuilding work. Scapa is now part of Chivas Brothers and additional refurbishment was carried out in 2005.

Scapa is now the only distillery with a Lomond still. This was created by Alistair Cunningham of Hiram Walker in 1955 with the aim of producing different types of whisky at a single distillery.

Scapa Flow is an interesting site for military naval historians, for during World War I the German naval fleet sought refuge there prior to a planned offensive, which never took place. The Germans deliberately sunk their own ships so that they wouldn't fall into enemy hands. Remains of the ships can still be seen showing above the waters of Scapa Flow. During World War II the battleship Royal Oak was hit by a German submarine in 1939 and it too has its final resting place in Scapa Flow.

SCAPA 14 YEAR OLD 40% (80°)

Color Light summer gold with hints of copper.

Nose Oak, malt, pear drops, hint of sea salt, and citrus.

Taste Complex with barley, creamy caramel, bitter hazelnuts and spice. A dry, bitter orange, yet smooth finish. This is a very distinctive single malt, which is well worth seeking out and enjoying.

SPEYBURN

Speyside

Speyburn Distillery
Rothes, Aberlour, Morayshire AB38 7AG
Tel: +44 1340 831213
www.inverhouse.com

OWNERS: INVER HOUSE DISTILLERS

FOUNDED: 1897

VISITOR CENTER: NO

Speyburn Distillery was founded in 1897 by John Hopkins & Co in a picturesque position, nestled in the rolling wooded hills of the Spey Valley. The company already owned Tobermory distillery, which they had purchased in 1890. The distillery was made from local stone and because it is in a valley it was built two and three storys high to take into account the climbing hillside behind. The location was chosen for its pure water source, the Granty Burn, and because it was close to the railroad.

Tradition has it that distillation started before the building work was completed and it was so cold that employees were forced to work in their overcoats. The reason being the directors wanted to commemorate Queen Victoria's Diamond Jubilee on November 1, 1897 with their first fillings, but in fact only one cask was bonded in 1897. Speyburn was one of the first malt distilleries to use pneumatic drum maltings, which were originally steam-driven. The drum maltings closed in 1968. There are just two stills at Speyburn and everything is very much as it was when the distillery was first built.

Speyburn was bought by Distillers Company Limited along with Tobermory in 1916. After various periods of closure Speyburn was purchased by Inver House Distillers in 1991.

Speyburn is a favorite single malt in the United States. Current bottlings include Speyburn 10, 16, 25, and 27 year old expressions.

SPEYBURN 10 YEAR OLD 40% (80°)

Color   Pale amber gold.

Nose   A dry, sweet-scented aroma.

Taste   A warm, flavorful malt with hints of honey and a herbal finish.

SPEYBURN 25 YEAR OLD 46% (92°)

Color   Pale amber with honey gold.

Nose   Light honey with almond marzipan and malt.

Taste   Warm caramel and cream, stewed plums, and a hint of cinnamon, dry finish with honeyed notes.

SPRINGBANK

Campbeltown

Springbank Distillery
Campbeltown, Argyll PA28 6EX
Tel: +44 1586 552085
www.springbankdistillers.com

OWNERS: J & A MITCHELL

FOUNDED: 1828

VISITOR CENTER: YES

Springbank was built in Campbeltown on the Mull of Kintyre, by brothers Archibald and Hugh Mitchell on the site of their father's illegal still. It is believed that the family had been distilling for at least 100 years before. By 1872 the Mitchell family owned four distilleries in the area. Demand for Campbeltown whisky continued to grow as it was much prized by blenders. A supply of local coal to fire the stills encouraged building and at one time there were more than 30 distilleries in Campbeltown. Unfortunately, with a few exceptions, distillers started to cut corners and the quality deteriorated. By the 1920s the blenders were starting to look elsewhere for fine malts.

The high standard of the Mitchell's single malt never altered and today Springbank whiskies are sought after by connoisseurs the world over. The company still belongs to the Mitchell brothers' descendants.

Springbank provides 100 percent of its malted barley on traditional floor maltings. Springbank also supplies malted barley for Longrow and Glengyle. Springbank has its own bottling line, and everything is controlled by the company. Springbank is a lightly peated malt 25ppmillion. Two other single malts whose recipes were retained after the distilleries closed are produced by Springbank. These are Hazelburn, which is triple distilled, and unpeated, and Longrow peated at 50ppmillion. Hazelburn was founded in 1796 and closed in 1925. Longrow distillery built in 1824 was located next door to Springbank and closed in 1896.

SPRINGBANK 10 YEAR OLD 46% (92°)

Color   Pale straw.

Nose   Honeyed vanilla, light smoke.

Taste   Light cream with hints of honey and sharpness in the dry, light smoke finish.

SPRINGBANK 15 YEAR OLD 46% (92°)

Color   Pale antique gold.

Nose   Fresh, rich with a hint of peat.

Taste   Medium-bodied with an initial sweetness followed by a taste of the sea, smoke, and oak with a long, smooth finish.

STRATHISLA

Speyside

Strathisla Distillery
Seafield Avenue, Keith, Banffshire AB55 3BS
Tel: +44 1542 783044
www.chivas.com

OWNERS: CHIVAS BROTHERS PERNOD RICARD

FOUNDED: 1786

VISITOR CENTER: YES

Strathisla distillery was founded as Milltown or Milton in 1786 by George Taylor and Alexander Milne. Records show that at this time Keith was well known for the linen produced at various mills. Water was in plentiful supply both from the River Isla which flows through Keith and from its many wells and natural springs. Water also provided one of the key raw materials for whisky production and, as elsewhere in Scotland, new distilleries were being built in and around Keith. The distillery was designed by John Alcock and is one of the most picturesque in Scotland and well worth a visit.

The distillery changed hands in 1825 and then in 1830 was purchased by William Longmore. He was a local merchant well respected in Keith and the distillery grew. In 1870 the name was changed to Strathisla. William died in 1882 and management of the distillery passed to his son-in-law John Geddes. Confusingly for history buffs, the distillery changed its name back to Milton in 1890. The next 50 years were unhappy ones for the distillery and by 1949 the business was bankrupt. The owner was George Pomeroy, a London financier who was found guilty of tax evasion.

Chivas Brothers bought the business at auction in 1950 and by 1951 it was again called Strathisla. Considerable restoration and major building work was started and the new visitor center, the home of Chivas Regal, built.

STRATHISLA OLD HIGHLAND MALT WHISKY
12 YEAR OLD 43% (86°)

Color   Warm coppery-gold.

Nose   Beautiful aroma full of summer fruit and flowers and malted barley.

Taste   Light on the tongue with hints of peat and caramel. Long, smooth fruity finish.

TALISKER

Isle of Skye/Highland

Talisker Distillery
Carbost, Skye IV47 8SR
Tel: +44 1478 614308
www.malts.com

OWNERS: DIAGEO

FOUNDED: 1830

VISITOR CENTER: YES

Talisker is the only distillery on the Island of Skye. Skye is the largest Inner Hebridean island and is well known for the Cuillins — a magnet for rock climbers, hill walkers, and mountaineers. Talisker comes from the Norse Thalas Ghair and means "sloping rock."

Talisker was built in 1830 on the edge of Loch Harport by Hugh and Kenneth MacAskill. They came from the Island of Eigg with their sheep and leased Macleod land around Talisker House. The MacAskills' decision to build a distillery did not meet with local approval from the Rev. Roderick Macleod, "one of the greatest curses that . . . could befall it or any other place."

In 1854 Kenneth MacAskill died and the North of Scotland Bank who held the lease sold the distillery to Donald MacLennan. He ran into difficulties and John Anderson of Glasgow took the distillery over in 1867. However, in 1879 John Anderson was sent to prison having sold whisky stocks that he didn't actually own.

The still house was destroyed by fire in 1960 and reopened two years later after exact copies of the stills had been built. Talisker distillery is unique, as the pipes running off the main stills are U-shaped to catch the vapor before being transferred to the five wooden worm tubs. These are located outside and because of the cold temperature the vapor condenses quickly back to spirit. A small secondary copper pipe transfers any vapor trapped in the U-shaped pipes back to the wash stills for a second distillation.

TALISKER CLASSIC MALTS SELECTION ™
10 YEAR OLD 45.8% (96°)

Color   Pale copper with oily legs.

Nose   Intense smoke, barbecue beef, iodine, spicy, and a hint of light caramel.

Taste   First notes are seaweed, salt sea brine reminiscent of smoked fish, hints of honey on the tongue, then pepper and light smoke.

TALISKER 175TH ANNIVERSARY BOTTLING
NO AGE STATEMENT 45.8% (96°)

Color   Very pale light straw.

Nose   Gentle aromas of citrus and hazelnuts.

Taste   An explosion of flavors, honeyed sweetness, smoke, pepper, and sea brine. Warm, yet dry finish.

TOBERMORY

Isle of Mull/Highland

Tobermory Distillery
Tobermory, Isle of Mull, Argyllshire PA75 6NR
Tel: +44 1688 302645
www.burnstewartdistillers.com

OWNERS: BURN STEWART DISTILLERS

FOUNDED: 1795

VISITOR CENTER: YES

The town of Tobermory, on the island of Mull, is beautiful with its little colored houses along the waters edge, pier, and moorings for yachts and fishing boats. The town is instantly recognizable to many children as *Balamory*, a favorite TV programme in the UK.

The distillery was founded in 1795 by John Sinclair a local merchant, but didn't become fully operational until 1823, when the land was granted to Sinclair by the British Society for Extending Fisheries and Improving the Sea Coasts of the Kingdom. The distillery was purchased by Distillers Company Limited in 1916 from John Hopkins & Co who owned it from 1890. In 1930 it closed and didn't reopen until 1972, when it was bought by a group of businesses and renamed Ledaig. This did not last long and it closed again in 1975. It was purchased in 1978 by the Kirkleavington Property Co of Cleckheaton in Yorkshire. A new company, Tobermory Distillers was formed and production started again in 1979. Finally after another closure the distillery was purchased by Burn Stewart in 1993.

Tobermory single malt is made from unpeated barley and is available at 10 years old. Some distillations are made using peated barley and these are bottled as Ledaig. There are several Ledaig expressions currently available, Legaid Unaged, Ledaig Sherry Finish, and Ledaig 10 year old, although distribution is restricted and it is not available worldwide.

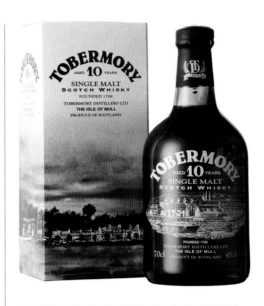

TOBERMORY 10 YEAR OLD 40% (80°)

Color   Pale summer gold.

Nose   The island in a bottle — a light, soft, heathery aroma with a hint of sea salt.

Taste   Medium bodied with malted barley wrapped in honey, summer herbs, and a luscious mouthfeel, warm sensuous finish.

LEDAIG 10 YEAR OLD 43% (86°)

Color   Pale lemon honey.

Nose   Musty, smoky, tarmac roads in the hot sun. With water opens up to reveal malted smoked barley notes.

Taste   Bitter almonds, charred wood, then hints of honey, dried raisins, and full-bodied smoke experience.

LEDAIG SHERRY 4 YEAR OLD 42% (84°)

Color   Golden sunshine.

Nose   Bonfires, coal tar, burned sugar, and malt.

Taste   Hint of bitter oranges and sweetness first, then charred barbecue smoke, lingering finish.

TOMATIN

Highland

Tomatin Distillery
Tomatin, Inverness-shire IV13 7YT
Tel: +44 1808 511444
www.tomatin.com

OWNERS: TOMATIN DISTILLERY CO
(MARUBENI EUROPE PLC)

FOUNDED: 1897

VISITOR CENTER: YES

Tomatin Distillery was founded in 1897 by the Tomatin-Spey District-Distillery Co Ltd, which went bankrupt in 1906. The distillery reopened in 1909 and the owners continued to increase the number of stills, until by 1974 there were a total of 23. Tomatin became the largest distillery in Scotland and only Hakushu in Japan exceeded its production. The owners' business failed in 1985 and the distillery was bought by two of its Japanese customers, Takara Shuzo and Okura. In 1997 the company purchased J. W. Hardie, owners of the Antiquary blended whisky. In 1998 Okura and Company sold their share to Takara Shuzo, now members of the Marubeni group.

The number of stills has been reduced by half and Tomatin is now the second largest distillery in Scotland, with Glenfiddich in first place.

Water for the distillery is provided by the Allt na Frithe Burn. The distillery is one of the highest in Scotland, 1,028 feet (312 meters) above sea level.

Tomatin is bottled by the company at 12, 18, and 25 years old. The main markets in terms of sales volume are Japan, USA, UK, France, and Denmark.

TOMATIN 12 YEAR OLD 40% (80°)

Color   Light summer gold with copper flashes.

Nose   Warm, malty, light heather honey with citrus.

Taste   Smooth and sweet for the honey note on the nose is the first thing that fills the mouth, medium bodied, malt, with a hint of citrus and licorice. A medium-length smooth, dry, smoky finish with a tingle.

TOMATIN 25 YEAR OLD 43% (86°)

Color   Pale summer gold.

Nose   A springtime youthful nose, apple blossom and soft fudge.

Taste   This was superb, Devon cream tea with honey, hint of tropical fruits, warm apricots, maybe a hint of cardamom and other exotic spices. A light, dry, spicy, long finish, an excellent dram.

TOMINTOUL

Speyside

Tomintoul Distillery
Ballindalloch, Banffshire AB37 9AQ
Tel: +44 1807 590274
www.tomintouldistillery.co.uk

OWNERS: ANGUS DUNDEE DISTILLERS	
FOUNDED: 1964	
VISITOR CENTER: No	

Tomintoul was one of the distilleries constructed in the 1960s to meet the rising demand for whisky for blending. Tomintoul was built in 1964 by a group of companies trading as the Tomintoul Distillery Ltd and production started in 1965. Tomintoul village is the highest in Scotland and in the heart of the countryside. In fact, the modern distillery looks a little out of place in this picturesque landscape. Water for Tomintoul comes from the Ballantruan spring, which rises in the Cromdale Hill.

It wasn't until 1972 that Tomintoul started to be sold as a single malt bottling.

The original owners sold the distillery to Scottish & Universal Investment Trust in 1973 who also bought Whyte & Mackay the same year. The company increased the number of stills from two to four in 1974. The distillery changed hands several times after that, along with the rest of the Whyte & Mackay portfolio. In 1996 JBB Greater Europe sold Tomintoul to Angus Dundee Distillers.

Tomintoul is available at 10, 16, and 27 years old and the company will be launching a Vintage 1976 bottling in 2007.

In celebration of the Ballantruan spring, Angus Dundee has launched Old Ballantruan. A peated Speyside single malt, which replicates the original smoky whiskies produced when peat was the most readily available fuel. Ballantruan is bottled at 50% (100°) and is unchillfiltered.

OLD BALLANTRUAN SPEYSIDE GLENLIVET UNCHILLFILTERED 50% (100°)

Color   Light gold.

Nose   Malt, old socks, light smoke with leather, and light floral notes lurking in the background.

Taste   Well balanced in the mouth, intermingling strands of peat, honey, and malt with a creamy finish.

TOMINTOUL 16 YEAR OLD 40% (80°)

Color   Warm chestnut gold.

Nose   Lemon apple strudel pancakes, vanilla, and a spice prickle.

Taste   Creamed apples, caramel, and warm spice coating the mouth with a dry slightly sharp finish.

TORMORE

Speyside

Tormore Distillery
Advie, Grantown-on-Spey, Moray PH26 3LR
Tel: +44 1807 510244
www.tormore.com

OWNERS: CHIVAS BROTHERS PERNOD RICARD

FOUNDED: 1959

VISITOR CENTER: No

Tormore can be described as a model distillery, being one of the first new ones to be built in the twentieth century in Scotland. Designed by Sir Alfred Richardson with whitewashed buildings and copper roofs, Tormore is constructed around a square complete with chiming clock and distillery worker's houses nearby. The distillery can clearly be seen from the road running between Grantown-on-Spey and Aberlour with a backdrop of pine-clad hills and landscaped gardens.

A short walk up behind the distillery leads to the water source where the pure clear spring water can be seen tumbling into a pool. If you are lucky enough to be invited here — there is no visitor center — see if you can take a dram of Tormore with you to the pool and drink it with a little of the water, which makes this fine single malt. It is a truly memorable experience.

It was built for Long John and was sold to Whitbread in 1975. In 1989 Allied Lyons purchased Whitbread's spirit division and in 2005 the distillery was bought by Chivas Brothers Pernod Ricard.

TORMORE 12 YEAR OLD 40% (80°)

Color   Golden sunshine.

Nose   Dry with a slightly nutty overtone and hint of citrus.

Taste   Soft on the tongue, a well defined medium-flavored whisky, with malted barley, hints of citrus and spice, and a long slightly honeyed finish.

TULLIBARDINE

Highland

Tullibardine Distillery
Stirling Street, Blackford, Perthshire PH4 1QG
Tel: +44 1764 682252
www.tullibardine.com

OWNERS: TULLIBARDINE DISTILLERY LTD

FOUNDED: 1949

VISITOR CENTER: YES

They were making beer here from the fifteenth century, so there is a tradition for producing alcohol at Tullibardine. In 1488 King James IV of Scotland was crowned and beer from the brewery served at his coronation. There was an earlier distillery nearby also named Tullibardine from 1814–1837. The present distillery was built by Delmé Evans and C. I. Barratt for the Tullibardine Distillery Ltd.

Invergordon Distillers purchased Tullibardine in 1971, which was then taken over by Whyte and Mackay. In June 2003 the distillery was bought by a group of businessmen including Douglas Ross and Michael Beamish. For Michael, who worked at Distillers Company Limited and Drambuie, and Douglas who worked at United Distillers, this was the perfect opportunity as they had long wanted to set up on their own.

As the distillery had been mothballed since 1994, stocks of old whiskies have to be used in current bottlings. The first bottling was a 10 year old 1993. New spirit came off the stills in 2004 and Michael and Douglas aim to release a 10 year old in 2014 to coincide with the Ryder Cup at nearby Gleneagles.

The distillery was sympathetically mothballed with a view to potentially re-starting it, so the transition period was reasonably short, although work was required to bring everything up to modern standards. Michael managed to persuade John Black, who had recently retired from Tormore to come and help out, and three years on he is still there!

TULLIBARDINE 1993 46% (92°)

Color   Pale summer gold.

Nose   Immediate Sherry notes with raisins, hint of leather, and smoke.

Taste   Fills the mouth with fruit and honey, back notes of blackcurrant and dried raisins. Long warm finish with malt and pepper spice overtones.

TULLIBARDINE PORT WOOD FINISH 1993, BOTTLED 2006 46% (92°)

Color   Warm gold with ruby flashes.

Nose   Deep, wet blackcurrant leaves, toasted hazelnuts, burned sugar, menthol, vanilla, pencil sharpenings.

Taste   Rich, blackberry and apple crumble, caramel hazelnut crunch, with a medium dry finish.

OTHER SCOTTISH SINGLE MALT DISTILLERIES

This section gives some information on 33 other Scottish distilleries. Most of these are not being actively promoted by their owners and some are silent at the time of writing this book in March 2007. The majority of distilleries that have closed forever, with a couple of exceptions, are excluded. There are also a couple of special malt bottlings included.

There are some new distilleries which are not featured, some have started producing, others have not yet laid the first foundation stone, such as Ladybank, Daftmill, and Blackfoot.

BURN STEWART DISTILLERS LTD (CL FINANCIAL)
www.burnstewartdistillers.com

DEANSTON
Founded 1965 in an old cotton mill dating from 1785, Deanston was purchased in 1990 by Burn Stewart Distillers. This distillery is the home of Scottish Leader, Burn Stewart's blended Scotch whisky. Deanston is available as a single malt at 12 years old.

DEANSTON 12 YEAR OLD 40% (80°)

Color   Pale amber.

Nose   A truly cereal aroma.

Taste   The malt flavor hits the palate first and then citrus and honey notes come into play.

CHIVAS BROTHERS PERNOD RICARD
www.chivas.com

ALT-A-BHAINE
Alt-a-Bhaine was founded in 1975 to provide malt whisky for the owner's blended whiskies. The distillery was mothballed in 2002, but reopened in 2005. Bottlings can be found from independent specialty bottlers such as Gordon & MacPhail and Signatory from time to time.

GLENALLACHIE
Founded 1967 and designed by William Delmé Evans, the famous distillery architect of the time. The distillery was closed in 1987 but reopened in 1989 when Pernod Ricard bought Glenallachie. A few bottlings are available from independent specialty bottlers.

GLENBURGIE
Glenburgie started life in 1810 and was built by William Paul as Kilnflat distillery. The distillery reopened as Glenburgie Glenlivet in 1878. In 1925 the distillery was managed by Margaret Nicol and she became managing director in 1930. Glenburgie is currently available from specialty bottlers such as Gordon & MacPhail. There was also a fabulous cask of Glenburgie which I launched as part of the Helen

Arthur Single Cask Collection in 2005. It sold so well that there are now no bottles left. Maybe I can persuade Chivas Brothers to start bottling this fine single malt themselves in the near future?

GLENTAUCHERS
Glentauchers was founded in 1897 by a partnership of W. P. Lowrie & Co Ltd blenders and James Buchanan & Co. The distillery produces malts primarily for blended whiskies and only small amounts are currently available from specialty bottlers.

MILTON DUFF
This distillery was founded in 1824 by Andrew Peary and Robert Bain, although it is certain that there were many distilleries in the Glen of Pluscarden before then. Lomond stills were installed in 1964 by the then owners Hiram Walker & Sons. A heavier malt whisky was produced called Mosstowie using these stills, which were removed in 1981.

The following distilleries are temporarily silent:

BRAEVAL (BRAES OF GLENLIVET)
Founded in 1973 by the Chivas Glenlivet group; Braeval is the highest distillery in Scotland at 1,100 feet (335 meters) above sea level.

CAPERDONICH
Founded in 1897 by Major James Grant, the owner of Glen Grant distillery and for many years known as Glen Grant No 2. It closed in 1902 and reopened in 1965 as Caperdonich after the well which supplies water to both distilleries.

GLEN KEITH
Founded in 1958, this Speyside distillery was one of the first to open in the twentieth century. Originally built for triple distillation. Glen Keith is available from specialty bottlers such as Duncan Taylor.

IMPERIAL
Imperial was founded in 1897 by Thomas Mckenzie who owned Dailuaine and Talisker. The distillery was forced to close following the Pattison whisky crash in 1899, but production started again in 1919. Occasionally, specialty bottlers such as Signatory release examples of Imperial. The distillery was recently sold and will close forever.

COORDINATED DEVELOPMENT SERVICES/ RAYMOND ARMSTRONG

www.bladnoch.co.uk

Scotland's most southerly distillery was founded in 1817 by Thomas McLelland. It remained in family ownership until it was sold to Dunville & Co of Belfast in 1911. After World War II the distillery closed and the equipment was dismantled and taken to Sweden. In 1956 the Baldnoch Distillery Co was established and new stills built. In 1993 Bladnoch closed and was bought for redevelopment by Raymond Armstrong, but the urge to recreate Bladnoch become too strong and distilling started again in 2000.

JOHN DEWAR & SONS/BACARDI

www.dewars.com

AULTMORE

Aultmore was founded in 1896 by Alexander Edward who owned Benrinnes and helped build Craigellachie distilleries. Aultmore comes from the Gaelic for "big burn" and sits alongside the Auchinderran Burn. In 1923 Aultmore was purchased by John Dewar & Sons Ltd. Aultmore is the smallest of Dewar's distilleries and its whisky is much sought after by blenders and whisky connoisseurs. Aultmore is available from the distillers at 12 years old and also from specialty bottlers.

AULTMORE 12 YEAR OLD 43% (86°)

Color   Pale gold.

Nose   Light, honey, citrus, malted barley.

Taste   Honey, citrus and a hint of spice with a short warm finish.

CRAIGELLACHIE

Craigellachie Distillery was founded in 1891 by Alexander Edward and Peter Mackie. Peter Mackie was one of the great whisky pioneers of the late nineteenth century and his name is synonymous with White Horse blended whisky, which was registered in 1890. Craigellachie was bought by John Dewar & Sons from United Distillers in 1998.

CRAIGELLACHIE 14 YEAR OLD 43% (86°)

Color   Medium gold.

Nose   Warm, intense barley and hint of smoke.

Taste   Complex with a real bite and a slightly bitter finish.

MACDUFF (GLEN DEVERON)

Macduff was founded in 1962 by the Duff family and others on the site by the banks of the River Deveron. Macduff single malt is sold under the Glen Deveron label when purchased from the distillery. If you should find a bottle of Macduff it will be from a specialty bottler, such as Douglas Laing's Platinum Range.

GLEN DEVERON 10 YEAR OLD 40% (80°)

Color   Warm summer gold.

Nose   Leather and oak reminiscent of a gentleman's library with a honeyed undernote.

Taste   Kumquat orange sharpness with cooked barley and a hint of creamy honey. Dry finish.

ROYAL BRACKLA

Founded 1812 by Captain William Fraser and built near Cawdor Castle, which is historically the home of Macbeth. Royal Brackla was the first distillery to have Royal added to its name. The others are Royal Lochnagar and Glenury Royal. William IV granted the Royal Warrant to the distillery in 1833. There are limited distillery bottlings of Royal Brackla available as well as those from independent specialty bottlers.

ROYAL BRACKLA 10 YEAR OLD 43% (86°)

Color   Warm gold with copper glints.

Nose   Caramelized oranges, malt, burned raisins.

Taste   Full bodied, burned caramel, cloves, bitter almonds, with a dry smoke finish.

DIAGEO

www.malts.com

Single malts from some of these distilleries were originally available as part of the Flora & Fauna and Rare Malt collections. Bottlings are sometimes available at distillery stores as part of the Distillery Malt Series in limited quantities. Production is mainly destined for blending.

AUCHROISK

Auchroisk was founded in 1974 by Justerini & Brooks to ensure a steady supply of malt for their blends. There are very few bottlings of Auchroisk available; in the past it was bottled more usually as The Singleton of Auchroisk.

BENRINNES

Founded 1834 by Peter McKenzie, although he had previously built a distillery in 1826 called Benrinnes some miles away. The new distillery was named Lyne of Ruthrie, but changed its name to Benrinnes several years later.

BLAIR ATHOL

Blair Athol was built in 1798 by John Stewart and Robert Robertson as Aldour. This is considered the home of Bell's whisky and its visitor center is to be recommended. Like many distilleries Blair Athol was run for a short time by a woman — Elizabeth Connacher from 1860 to 1882, which clearly commends it to the author! Visitor center telephone number + 44 1796 482003.

DAILUAINE

Dailuaine was founded 1852 by William Mackenzie. There is no visitor center here, but if you are driving by look out for the pagoda roof; this is the first one built by the famous distillery architect Charles Doig.

DUFFTOWN

The Dufftown-Glenlivet Distillery Co was founded in 1896 when the distillery was built inside an old meal mill. The original water wheel is still at the site. Dufftown was the sixth distillery to be built in the town after Mortlach (1823), Glenfiddich (1886), Balvenie (1892), Convalmore (1894-1985), and Parkmore (1894-1931).

On August 23, 2006, Diageo released The Singleton of Dufftown in selected duty free outlets. The bottling is in a nineteenth century style blue glass flask with distinctive labeling and packaging. The idea of The Singleton brand name, which has been used with other Diageo bottlings, is to "help consumers to more easily recognise The Singleton of Dufftown as a single malt Scotch whisky."

GLENDULLAN

Founded in 1897, this was the last distillery to be built in Dufftown in the nineteenth century. Glendullan shared a private siding off the Great North of Scotland Railway with Mortlach distillery. There are occasional distillery bottlings of this single malt.

GLEN SPEY

Glen Spey was founded in 1878 as the Mill of Rothes distillery by James Stuart & Co to provide single malt for J&B blended whiskies. There is a 12 year old Glen Spey available from the distillery and also occasionally from independent specialty bottlers.

INCHGOWER

Inchgower was built in 1871 by Alexander Wilson to replace Tochineal distillery, which had also been built by him in 1832. The business went into liquidation and was purchased by Arthur Bell & Sons in 1938. Inchgower can be found from independent specialty bottlers.

MANNOCHMORE

Founded in 1971 on the same site as Glenlossie to create increased capacity for blended whiskies owned by the group. In 1996 a dark Mannochmore was released called Loch Dhu. Production has since stopped, but you may find a bottle somewhere.

MORTLACH

Mortlach was founded in 1823 by James Findlater and the first to be constructed in Dufftown. This distillery produces a fine single malt and there are a few specialty bottlings available, including one from The Helen Arthur Single Cask Collection. The stillroom has three wash and three spirit stills, which are completely different from each other, making it one of the hardest distilleries to run.

PORT ELLEN

Port Ellen was founded in 1825 as a malt mill by Alexander Mackay and Walter Campbell. After a few changes of ownership in quick succession, John Ramsay came over from Glasgow. He quickly found a market for Port Ellen in North America and negotiated to export whisky in larger casks, which were stored in duty free warehouses before despatch. When Ramsay died in 1892, his wife Lucy inherited Port Ellen. She ran the distillery until her death in 1906 when it passed to her son, Captain Iain Ramsay. Port Ellen Distillery was closed permanently in 1987, but luckily for single malt lovers and Islay aficionados in particular there was plenty of stock. Today, Port Ellen is the home to the maltings for all of the distilleries on the Island of Islay.

Port Ellen is part of Diageo's Special Releases programme and includes a Port Ellen 27 year old from 2006, a Port Ellen 25 year old from 2005, and another Port Ellen 25 year old in 2004.

STRATHMILL

Founded in 1891 this was one of the earliest single malts to be marketed in 1909. However, for most of its life Strathmill has been an important single malt for major blends. Occasionally independent bottlings are released.

TEANINICH

Teaninich was built in 1817 by Captain Hugh Munro. Teaninich is a distinctive single malt, which is produced slightly differently from others as mash filters are used after the grist has been mixed with water.

EDRINGTON GROUP

GLENTURRET

www.famousgrouse.co.uk
Founded 1775, Glenturret is Scotland's oldest highland malt whisky distillery. There were several silent periods, so the accolade of Scotland's oldest highland distillery in continuous production in fact goes to Strathisla, which was built in 1786. Glenturret is home to The Famous Grouse Experience and because of its close proximity to Edinburgh, is one of the most visited distilleries in Scotland. Visitor center telephone number + 44 1764 656565.

TAMDHU

Founded in 1896 Tamdhu distillery was built by a group of whisky blenders with William Grant. Tamdhu is one of the few distilleries to have its own Saladin maltings and these provide all the malted barley required for distillation at Tamdhu and much of Glen Rothes.

The following distillery was mothballed in 1986.

GLENGLASSAUGH

Built in 1873 by a group of businessmen, Glenglassaugh was renovated by one of them, Alexander Morrison, in 1887. He sold the distillery to customers Robertson & Baxter in 1892. The distillery was closed several times after that and after rebuilding reopened in 1960 only to close again 26 years later.

FORTUNE BRANDS (BEAM GLOBAL UK)

ARDMORE

Founded 1898. Built by William Teacher & Sons in Kennethmont, near Huntly, Aberdeenshire. The bulk of the distillery's production is destined for blended whisky, in particular Teacher's Highland Cream. Special bottlings are sometimes available.

WILLIAM GRANT

KININVIE

Kininvie was founded in 1990 by William Grant & Sons Ltd, owners of Glenfiddich and Balvenie to provide additional single malt whisky for their own blended whiskies.

MONKEY SHOULDER (NOT A DISTILLERY)

www.monkeyshoulder.com.
Monkey Shoulder is a triple malt Scotch whisky, developed by David Stewart, Master Distiller at William Grant. The first thing you notice is the distinctive bottle, which is shaped a little like the squat Balvenie, but has three monkeys crawling along one shoulder. The name is said to come from the temporary sprain in one shoulder created by consistently turning over the barley on the malting floors — something which, of course, Wm Grant & Sons still do — so they should know.

Monkey Shoulder has been developed by Wm Grant & Sons to bring single malts to a wider audience — it's never too late to try something new — and to show how good whisky can be as a mixer.

INVER HOUSE DISTILLERS

www.inverhouse.com

BALMENACH

As the dust settled after the introduction of the 1823 Excise Act, James MacGregor applied for a license for his farm distillery. Balmenach has changed hands frequently and was mothballed in 1993 until Inver House bought it in 1997.

AULLOCH LOMOND DISTILLERY CO

GLEN SCOTIA

Founded in 1832 by the Galbraith family. This is one of the few Campbeltown distilleries left from the great years of the late nineteenth and early twentieth centuries. For example, 17 Campbeltown distilleries closed between 1920 and 1934.

LOCH LOMOND

Founded in 1965 by Duncan Thomas and American Barton Brands. The distillery was bought by Glen Catrine Bonded Warehouse Ltd in 1985. There are various bottlings from the distillery with different characteristics, some little peated, others highly peated, for example Old Rhosdhu, Inchmurrin, Inchmoan, Craiglodge, and Croftenga.

J & A MITCHELL

GLENGYLE

In April 2004 this Campbeltown distillery was reborn and the new spirit will become whisky in April 2007. Glengyle was founded by William Mitchell in 1872, but closed in 1925, although its name lives on as a Blended Malt. New bottlings will be released as Kilkerran. I had the privilege of tasting a "work in progress" sample of Kilkerran, a lightly peated single malt that is double distilled. The sample comes from a Sherry cask. I look forward to tasting Kilkerran in a few years' time; it promises to be a very good whisky.

KILKERRAN CASK SAMPLE 2004 SHERRY BUTT 58.6% (117.2°)

Color   Light summer gold.

Nose   Malt, light smoke.

Taste   First notes are creamy, malt, honey, and smoke, surprisingly rounded for such a young single malt. The finish is slightly bitter, dry, and long.

MORRISON BOWMORE

MCCLELLAND'S – NOT A DISTILLERY BUT A RANGE OF SINGLE MALT SCOTCH WHISKIES

The McClelland's range is designed to illustrate the four key whisky distilling regions – Islay, Lowland, Speyside, and Highland. There is also a McClelland's Highland Sherry Finished 12 year old and McClelland's Highland 16 year old.

SPEYSIDE DISTILLERS

www.speysidedistillery.co.uk

SPEYSIDE

Founded in 1962 as the result of one man's dream to build his own distillery, George Christie. Speyside distillery is now owned by a group of investors including Ricky Christie. Speyside is marketed as Drumguish unaged and Speyside 8 and 10 year old expressions. The company markets a variety of other special bottlings such as Glentromie Blended Malt and blends including Scott's Selection.

WHYTE AND MACKAY LIMITED

www.whyteandmackay.co.uk

FETTERCAIRN

Founded in 1824, the building was originally a corn mill, which was destroyed by fire in 1887. Old Fettercairn is available at 12 years old. Fettercairn has a good visitor center and as the distillery is one of the few on the east coast of Scotland is a good place to remember when planning your itinerary. Visitor center Tel: +44 (0) 1561 340205.

TAMNAVULIN

As I write in March 2007, I am delighted to hear that this distillery will soon be reopened. Tamnavulin was built in 1966 by a subsidiary of Invergordon Distillers Ltd. Whyte & Mackay bought Invergordon in 1993 and with several company name changes is still part of the group. The distillery closed in 1995. Whyte & Mackay have released several expressions of Tamnavulin recently.

BLENDED SCOTCH WHISKIES

The art of blending does not solely apply to the whisky industry. Tea, coffee, and perfumes, for example, are also blended and rely on the olfactory senses of a master blender.

Blends are often overlooked by the consumer today in the hype created by the single malt connoisseur. This is unforgivable, for the art of blending is highly skilled. In the key whisky producing countries, blenders are masters of their craft with a finely tuned sense of smell and taste and the ability to create great blends from a wide choice of whiskies. It is also true that without the blending industry, single malt whiskies would not survive. About 96 percent of all single malt production is destined for the blenders. Today, blended whisky still accounts for some 90 percent of total sales worldwide.

Blends can be produced using a selection of single malts only — these are called pure malt or vatted malt whiskies. For the most part, blends in Scotland and other countries such as Japan are defined as a mix of single malt and grain whiskies. To qualify as Blended Scotch Whiskies the single malt and grain whiskies used must always be produced in Scotland. Irish, American, and Canadian blends are created using whiskies produced from different grains.

In some cases blends were created around a single malt, for example Teacher's Ardmore, Johnnie Walker's Cardhu, and Lang's Glengoyne. The secret was to marry these core single malts with others and grain whisky to create a harmonious whole. Today, the onus is on the master blenders to recreate the essence of a blend with each bottling. This is not easy as once a bottle is opened changes occur, so the aromas, tastes, and mouthfeel of a blend can only properly be stored in the master blenders' memory, not in a reference sample.

In emerging markets, blends had a shaky start for early products weren't really whisky at all. Often they were made from distillates of dubious heritage and yeast extract and caramel added to give a "whisky" feel to the product.

Joint venture companies in, for example, India and China, with leading Scotch whisky groups have been a major building block on the road to producing good quality blends.

The whiskies in this section are all Scottish blends. It is by no means a definitive list; space simply doesn't allow for this and there are literally thousands of different brand names marketed worldwide.

THE ANTIQUARY

www.antiquary.co.uk

OWNERS: TOMATIN DISTILLERY CO LTD
MARKETED THROUGH J & W HARDIE LTD
COMPANY FOUNDED: 1861

Antiquary was created by J & W Hardie Ltd, a company established at 4 Picardy Place, Edinburgh in 1861. J & W Hardie Ltd were the original licensees of the Benromach Distillery and shareholders (1887) in North British Distillery. In 1917 Antiquary was taken over by J & G Stewart, Edinburgh wine and tea merchants. In time both companies became part of Distillers Company Ltd and the brand reverted to J & W Hardie. Antiquary was purchased along with J & W Hardie Ltd by Tomatin Distillery Co Ltd in 1995.

Antiquary is named after a novel by Sir Walter Scott (1771–1832), Scottish novelist and collector of old Scottish ballads.

Antiquary is available as Antiquary Finest, Antiquary 12, and Antiquary 21 year old.

THE ANTIQUARY FINEST 40% (80°)

Color   Pale summer gold.

Nose   Almond, light caramel, and vanilla.

Taste   Light, honey, hints of creamed almond nougat, and a dry finish.

THE ANTIQUARY 21 YEAR OLD 43% (86°)

Color   Amber gold.

Nose   Honey, grain, light vanilla.

Taste   Grain flavors are the first to hit the tongue with burned caramel, then the malt comes through, a long recurring many-layered finish.

BAILIE NICOL JARVIE

www.glenmorangie.com

OWNERS: THE GLENMORANGIE CO
(MOËT HENNESSY)
COMPANY FOUNDED: 1921 (PROBABLY EARLIER)

Bailie Nicol Jarvie (BNJ) is named after a character from Sir Walter Scott's novel *Rob Roy*. Sir Walter Scott was born in 1771 and died in 1832. He first collected old Scottish ballads and became famous for his epic poems *Marmion* and *The Lady of the Lake* and Waverley series of Scottish novels.

BNJ was bought by Macdonald & Muir of Leith in 1923 from Nicol, Anderson and Co, a company also based in Edinburgh's port of Leith at Queen's Dock. Other whisky brand names purchased at the time included Souter Johnnie, Old Oak Tree, and Dunvegan. BNJ is an individual blended whisky which uses a small, select group of single malts including Glenmorangie and Glen Moray — 60% malt and 40% grain.

BNJ 40% (80°)
The following tasting notes are from BNJ.

Color   Pale gold.

Nose   Sweet and well-balanced, notes of vanilla, pears, and possibly violets, some nuts and fresh hay.

Taste   A full flavor, well balanced with a good body and a very slight trace of smoke. Every bit as mouth-watering on the palate as the nose suggests, with some lemon tartness countering the rich maltiness and almost chewable grain.

Finish   Warm, balanced, with a whiff of smoke. Very long for such a fragile blend, with an astonishing depth of simple malt and toffee.

BALLANTINE'S

www.chivas.com

OWNERS: CHIVAS BROTHERS PERNOD RICARD

COMPANY FOUNDED: 1827

BLEND FIRST LAUNCHED: 1879

In 1827 George Ballantine, the son of a Peeblesshire farmer, completed his five year apprenticeship with Andrew Hunter, a grocer and spirit dealer in Edinburgh. He was only 18, but decided to launch out on his own. By 1836 he had moved into larger premises at 67, South Bridge as "Wine Merchants and Grocers" and he had already started selling whiskies.

George married Isabella Mann in 1842 and they had three sons, Archibald, George, and Daniel. Together George and his sons created a large business and subsequently opened another branch in Glasgow.

In 1879 an article in a Glasgow newspaper said that George Ballantine & Son had, "cultivated a high reputation as blenders of fine old Highland whisky." This heralded a period of expansion and in 1881 George opened Ballantine's Blended Stores and Export Bottling Vaults at Granton, near Edinburgh. When George died in 1891 age 82, he left his sons a very healthy business with 20,000 gallons (90,900 liters) of whisky maturing in bond.

In 1895 Queen Victoria awarded George Ballantine & Son with a Royal Warrant, and the warrant continued in 1906 when King Edward VII came to the throne.

Ballantine's warehouses are patrolled by a very different type of security guard. For these guards do not wear navy uniforms and carry radios — they are a flock of geese and are known as "Ballantine's Scotch Watch."

Today, Ballantine's is one of the world's leading brands with two bottles being sold every second.

BALLANTINE'S FINEST 40% (80°)

Color   Summer hay with green highlights.

Nose   Pear drops, banana, malt, and smoke.

Taste   Creamy honey with light smoke and grain, short smoke finish with honey coating.

BELL'S

www.bells.co.uk

**BELL'S EXTRA SPECIAL
8 YEAR OLD 40% (80°)**

Color   Pale gold.

Nose   Smooth with a warm nutty aroma.

Taste   Medium bodied with a hint of spice
        and honey, fades away in the finish.

OWNERS: DIAGEO

COMPANY FOUNDED: 1825

BLEND FIRST LAUNCHED: 1904

Along with many other famous Scotch whisky blends, the story of Bell's started in a small store in Perth. In this case, the store opened in 1825, trading in tea and whisky. As the company website states, "At the time, they were oddly similar: both were precious commodities, highly taxed and kept in secure bonded warehouses."

Arthur Bell became a partner in the company in 1850. He started looking at blended whiskies, which were gaining popularity. Arthur started buying stocks of good whiskies for his customers and for the company's expanding blended whisky. The growth of the railroad system in Scotland meant that stocks could be delivered quickly to the new markets opening up in England.

Arthur died in 1900 and left his business to his sons.

In 1904 the name Arthur Bell & Sons first appeared on a label, and this showed a curler throwing a stone. Curling is a traditional Scottish game usually played on ice, which closely resembles bowls and is also popular in the United States, Canada, and Nordic countries.

In 1933 Bell's purchased Blair Athol and Dufftown-Glenlivet distilleries. In 1985 the company lost its independence and was purchased by Guinness, subsequently United Distillers.

BLACK BOTTLE

www.blackbottle.com

OWNERS: BURN STEWART DISTILLERS LTD

COMPANY FOUNDED: 1850

BLEND FIRST LAUNCHED: 1879

Black Bottle Original Blended Scotch Whisky started life, as did so many other brands, in a tea merchant's. The Victorian era was a time of growth and enterprise. The story begins with brothers David & Gordon Graham, the sons of a shoemaker in Torphins, a village near Aberdeen. In 1850 they came to Aberdeen to seek their fortunes in a busy port where goods were traded from around the world. They opened an office in Union Street and started trading in tea and blending tea for their customers.

By 1879 they had also gained a reputation for blending whisky and Black Bottle was born. In 1881 they decided to concentrate on whisky and stopped dealing in tea. They moved offices to Market Street and built two bonded warehouses in Regent Street.

Unfortunately, Gordon, who had been the designer of the brand, died in 1889 just as sales of Black Bottle were taking off; but the company's future seemed assured. In 1898 Pattisons, the large whisky brokers, went bankrupt and with them many leading blenders and distilleries of the time, however, the Graham brothers were able to ride out the storm. After World War I the black glass bottle became green, although the pot-still shape was retained.

The business remained in the family and was taken over by a nephew in 1955. In 1964 the business was sold to Long John and the brand suffered from a number of changes of ownership. It is now part of Burn Stewart Distillers and the company is reviving the brand. Black Bottle is a blend with a large proportion of Islay single malts.

BLACK BOTTLE ORIGINAL BLENDED SCOTCH WHISKY 40% (80°)

Color   Pale gold.

Nose   Smoke, smooth grain and malt notes with a hint of honey.

Taste   Peat smoke and honey mingle on the tongue, a punchy smoke finish with bittersweet citrus and honey.

CHIVAS REGAL

www.chivasregal.com

OWNERS: CHIVAS BROTHERS PERNOD RICARD

COMPANY FOUNDED: 1841

BLEND FIRST LAUNCHED: 1909

James Chivas worked in a grocery store on King Street, Aberdeen for William Edward. When Mr Edward died in 1841, James continued with a new partner Charles Stewart. The grocer's store offered a wide range of goods as an advertisement testified, "curious brandies, French liqueurs, green and dried fruits, teas as imported, hams, tongues, cheese, pickles and fish sauces, wax and sperm candles." James was eager to expand the business and started specializing in Scotch whiskies with an own blend Royal Glendee. He bought stocks of the finest whiskies he could source and laid them down, for he had a dream — to create the finest blended Scotch whisky.

By 1843 the company received the Royal Warrant from HM Queen Victoria, the first of many for the next 112 years. In 1857 the partnership with Charles Stewart was dissolved and James persuaded his brother John to join him. Sadly John died in 1862 but the business continued as Chivas Brothers.

In 1866 James died and the business was taken over by his son Alexander. Alexander died, age only 37, in 1893 and the company's clerk Alexander Smith together with Charles Stewart Howard continued the Chivas Brothers' pioneering work. In 1909 James' dream came true when Chivas Regal blended whisky was launched.

The company's growth was dramatic and the brand continued to sell in spite of two World Wars and Prohibition. Today over 3.9 million 9-liter cases of Chivas Regal are sold annually.

CHIVAS REGAL 12 YEAR OLD 40% (80°)

Color   Warm amber gold.

Nose   Intense summer fruits, hint of butterscotch, and slightly bitter notes

Taste   In the mouth the summer fruits mingle with malt and grain.

CHIVAS REGAL 18 YEAR OLD 40% (80°)

This has two single malts at its heart, Strathisla and Longmorn.

Color   Warm amber gold.

Nose   The summer fruits are here too with burned caramel and dark chocolate.

Taste   Full bodied, chocolate, bitter almonds, caramel, and apple pie, a long, rather dry finish.

CUTTY SARK

www.cutty-sark.com

OWNERS: BERRY BROS & RUDD LTD

COMPANY FOUNDED: 1698

BLEND FIRST LAUNCHED: 1923

The name Cutty Sark is synonymous with the tea trade in British history, as it was the name of the world's fastest and most famous clipper ship, built in Scotland. However, the origins of Cutty Sark are older than that, as it was the name for a short shirt worn by a witch in Robbie Burns poem *Tam O Shanter*. The witch was beautiful and could run like the wind.

Today, Cutty Sark represents one of the world's leading blended whiskies.

The first bottle and front and back labels were designed by James McBey and remain virtually unchanged. The composition of the blend also remains the same, with an emphasis on Speyside single malts.

Cutty Sark was launched by the directors of Berry Bros & Rudd in 1923 during Prohibition in the United States. Their reasons were perfectly clear. They wanted to produce a top quality whisky, which would be instantly recognized as genuine. Cutty Sark is light in color and was one of the first natural whiskies bottled without added caramel.

Sales of Cutty Sark took off in spite of the fact that Prohibition continued for another seven years. Berry Bros & Rudd, like most whisky merchants and distillers, were loathe to be seen openly exporting to the United States. However they were prepared to deliver cases to Nassau in Bahamas and didn't ask questions. Their agent in Nassau was a Captain William McCoy, a well-known smuggler and the phrase "the real McCoy" was coined.

CUTTY SARK BLENDED SCOTCH WHISKY 40% (80°)

Color   Pale straw.

Nose   Smooth grain and malt with pear drops, violets, light floral notes.

Taste   Smooth grain replicated in the mouth with light honey, apricots, apple puree, grassy with a hint of smoke.

CUTTY SARK 25 YEAR OLD 45.7% (91.4°)

Color   Medium gold with copper.

Nose   Powerful chestnut honey with vanilla and dried prunes.

Taste   Warm medium bodied, honey, oak wood characteristics and flavors reinforcing the grain and malt notes.

DEWAR'S WHITE LABEL

www.dewarsworldofwhisky.com

OWNERS: JOHN DEWAR & SONS/BACARDI

COMPANY FOUNDED: 1846

BLEND FIRST LAUNCHED: 1906 (BRAND NAME FIRST REGISTERED 1891)

John Dewar was born near Aberfeldy in Perthshire in 1806. On leaving school he was apprenticed to a joiner in Weem, and five years later moved back to Aberfeldy and worked for his brother James in his joinery business. Two years later he headed for Perth to start work with his uncle James MacDonald in his wine and spirit business. On James Macdonald's death in 1837, John became a partner and stayed there until 1846 when he set up his own wine and spirit merchant's in Perth.

The business grew and in 1860 the first traveling salesman was appointed. In 1871 John's eldest son joined the business age 15 and became a partner in 1879. John senior was not very well at the time and in 1880 he died at the age of 74. John junior took control and asked his youngest brother Thomas (Tommy) who worked in Leith for a whisky company to join him. Tommy became a partner in 1885.

Together the brothers were to transform their father's small wine and spirits merchant to become a public company. Tommy was the driving force and he moved to open offices in London. The company was awarded a Royal Warrant by Queen Victoria and this has been awarded by every monarch since. Tommy started traveling abroad and recorded his sales trips in *A Ramble Round the Globe*.

Dewar's White Label was created by the company's first blender, A. J. Cameron, in 1906. There are up to 40 different malt and grain Scotch whiskies in Dewar's White Label with Aberfeldy Single Malt a key ingredient.

DEWAR'S WHITE LABEL 40% (80°)

Color   Pale gold.

Nose   Citrus, light smoke, intense grain aromas.

Taste   Hint of honey, citrus prickle, robust grain flavors, and smooth malt.

J&B (JUSTERINI & BROOKS)

www.diageo.com

OWNERS: DIAGEO

COMPANY FOUNDED: 1750S

BLEND FIRST LAUNCHED: J & B "CLUB" SCOTCH 1880S

The story of Justerini & Brooks is a little different from the tales of the other whisky dynasties, for the hero is Italian rather than Scottish. Giacomo Justerini arrived in England in 1749 because he had fallen in love with an opera singer whom he followed to London. He had very little in his pocket apart from some gold and a notebook with recipes for spirit distillation from his uncle, who owned a distillery in Bologna. It seems that the opera singer, Margherita Bellino, was not totally immune to Giacomo's attentions and she introduced him to Samuel Johnson, whose nephew George, wanted to set up a business. The company Johnson and Justerini began trading with Giacomo's liqueurs and wines. These were turbulent times with the start of The Seven Years War in 1756, but the business grew and the two young men became rich.

By 1760 Giacomo decided to retire back home. History doesn't relate whether he in fact married Margherita but it is reasonable to assume that he didn't. Samuel made his son Augustus a partner in the business. The company's first advertisments to include whisky were in 1780.

The Johnson family continued to run the business until it was sold to Alfred Brooks in 1831 and the name was changed to Justerini and Brooks. J & B is bottled using more than 40 single malts including Knockando, Auchroisk, Glen Spey, and Strathmill.

J & B is the No 1 Scotch whisky in Europe and the No 2 in the world.

J & B RARE 40% (80°)

Color   Pale lemon straw.

Nose   Light, soft with Speyside malts and rich caramel undertones.

Taste   Vanilla and malt fill the mouth with plenty of character and a fresh finish.

JOHNNIE WALKER

www.johnniewalker.com

OWNERS: DIAGEO

COMPANY FOUNDED: 1820S

BLEND FIRST LAUNCHED: 1867

The story begins in 1805 with the birth of John Walker on a farm at Todriggs. His father Alexander died unexpectedly in 1815 and John was too young to take over the tenancy, so everything was sold. The Trustees of Alexander's estate started a small grocer's store in Kilmarnock in 1820 for John to manage. Like many of the other whisky legends, John's store sold a range of goods including tea, wines, and spirits. As good quality grain spirit became available and single malt whiskies improved, John started creating his own blends. When John died in 1857, his son Alexander took over the grocery business.

Alexander was only 20 when his father died, but within the next 30 years he was to turn the company into an international business. The key to the company's success was Walker's Old Highland Whisky, which was copyrighted in 1867. The original label was similar to the black and gold slanted design we know today for Johnnie Walker Black Label. The signature square bottle was introduced in the 1870s. The striding man logo created by Tom Browne, however, didn't appear until 1909. This is now probably one of the best known advertising logos in the world.

Alexander died in 1889 and by then his three sons, Jack, George, and Alexander were in the business. Sadly Jack died at only 21 while working in Australia. Together George and Alexander took over the business from their father's partners and despite various financial setbacks turned Walker's Old Highland Whisky into an internationally known brand.

JOHNNIE WALKER RED LABEL 40% (80°)

Color   Pale honey gold.

Nose   Smoke, malt, and fruit.

Taste   A full-flavored malty blend with honey and smoke and a long finish.

LANGS

www.ianmacleod.com

OWNERS: IAN MACLEOD DISTILLERS LIMITED

COMPANY FOUNDED: 1860S

BLEND FIRST LAUNCHED: 1861

Hugh Lang was born in Glasgow in 1802. In the 1860s Hugh Lang and his three sons ran a public house in Glasgow's port area of Broomielaw. The city of Glasgow was booming and the docks were at the heart of this expansion. Publicans often created their own blends and sold them to customers in large stone jars. Lang's whisky gained a loyal clientele from the sailors who frequented their inn and local dock workers.

In order to secure the future of their business, the Langs raised £100,000 through selling shares to members of the public. While Langs grew, another blending and broking company, William Robertson, was set up in Glasgow. The two companies were to work together for many years. The Langs started blending their own whiskies in the celler of a former Argyll Free Church at 16, Oswald Street, Glasgow. To gain access to one of their key single malts, Langs purchased Glengoyne Distillery in 1876. The company created a bonded warehouse by taking over the whole of the church in 1893. William Robertson bought Langs, in 1965 and together they become members of the Edrington Group.

Langs were awarded a Royal Warrant as whisky suppliers to HM Queen Elizabeth the Queen Mother in 1984.

Langs was purchased from Edrington by Ian Macleod Distillers Limited, along with Glengoyne Distillery, in 2003.

Langs is available as Langs Select and Langs Supreme blended whiskies.

LANGS SUPREME 5 YEAR OLD 40% (80°)

Color   Pale gold.

Nose   Citrus, fruity, crisp, and malty.

Taste   Light malt and grain well integrated in spite of this whisky's youthfulness, a short finish with honey and spice.

J & A MITCHELL

www.springbankdistillers.com

OWNERS: J & A MITCHELL

COMPANY FOUNDED: 1828

This entry is a little different to the rest of the chapter. The reason is simple. J & A Mitchell, distillers of Springbank, Longrow, Hazelburn, and Kilkerran, also produce a wide range of blends, which they market themselves. The blends are designed to reflect the illustrious history of the Campbeltown region, which at its height was the whisky capital of Scotland.

These blends are not available worldwide. They are sold mainly in the UK and France, with Campbeltown Loch 21 year old sold in Japan and Mitchell's 12 year old in Taiwan.

CAMPBELTOWN LOCH 21 YEAR OLD 40% (80°)

Color   Pale straw.

Nose   Wonderful soft aromas malt and grain, oak, honey, hint of smoke.

Taste   Gentle honey wraps around the mouth then citrus and smoke come through, lingering finish.

MITCHELL'S 12 YEAR OLD 43% (86°)

Color   Pale straw.

Nose   Smoke, salt spray, oak.

Taste   Creamy malt enfolds smooth smoke, sea salt prickle and an intense, long finish.

ROYAL SALUTE

www.chivas.com

OWNERS: CHIVAS BROTHERS PERNOD RICARD

COMPANY FOUNDED: 1841

Royal Salute was conceived by Chivas Brothers Master Blender, Colin Scott, to celebrate the coronation of HM Queen Elizabeth II in 1953. A 21-gun royal salute is traditionally fired from Royal Navel ships at such occasions. Royal Salute is a premium brand from Chivas Brothers, building on the success of their own brand and the remarkable inventory of fine whiskies laid down from the nineteenth century.

For example, Royal Salute The Hundred Cask Selection is created from a limited release of 100 casks. Royal Salute 50 year old is only available as a limited edition of 255 bottles created from whiskies matured for a minimum of 50 years.

The Royal Salute 21 year old is presented in a porcelain flagon, which shows Robert the Bruce and the Gaelic words which translate into "fidelity, stability since 1801," in a velvet pouch.

ROYAL SALUTE 21 YEAR OLD 40% (80°)

Color   Pale gold.

Nose   Warm caramel and smoke in light apple syrup.

Taste   A rich blend of oaky vanilla, malt, and sensuous grain whiskies.

SCOTTISH LEADER

www.scottishleader.com

OWNERS: BURN STEWART DISTILLERS LTD

BRAND FIRST LAUNCHED: LATE 19TH CENTURY

In 1817 the Ross brothers founded a grocer's and wine and spirits store in Dumbarton, which is a town on the Clyde close to Glasgow. Glasgow was rapidly expanding and the Ross brothers grew with the city. By 1860 the brothers were also dealing and blending whisky. The company was purchased by whisky brokers, the Burn Stewart Group in 1988 when the group was formed. Burn Stewart is a Glasgow-based company with three single malt distilleries; Deanston in Perthshire, Bunnahabhain on Islay, and Tobermory on the Isle of Mull.

Deanston is the key single malt at the heart of all Scottish Leader bottlings. The label was designed by Scottish artist Andrew Taylor and shows an Imperial stag with a tremendous set of antlers sitting at the foot of Ben Ledi, which positions the brand close to Deanston distillery.

The Scottish Leader brand includes a Blend of grain and malt whiskies and a Blended Malt. The current bottlings are Scottish Leader Blended Malt 14 year old and Scottish Leader Blended Malt (no age statement). Other bottlings are available from time to time.

SCOTTISH LEADER 14 YEAR OLD MALT 40% (80°)

Color   Warm gold.

Nose   Scented summer flowers on a hot day, hint of Sherry notes, oak, and leather.

Taste   Licorice, toffee, spice, dry light smoke finish.

TEACHER'S HIGHLAND CREAM

www.teacherswhisky.com

TEACHER'S HIGHLAND CREAM 40% (80°)

Color Deep honey gold.

Nose Warm, caramel, spice with a hint of smoke.

Taste Waves of flavor from the sherried single malts and smoother grain elements, spicy on the tongue with a long, comforting finish.

OWNERS: FORTUNE BRANDS/BEAM GLOBAL SPIRITS

COMPANY FOUNDED: 1856

BLEND FIRST LAUNCHED: 1884

William Teacher was born in 1811 at a time when life was tough for people in Scotland. The Napoleonic Wars (1803-1815) and the grain blockade imposed by the French meant that food was scarce. William started working with his mother in the local linen mill, but by 1830 he was in Glasgow working for Mrs. McDonald in her grocer's store and had already diversified into wines and spirits.

William married Mrs. McDonald's daughter Agnes and within a few years they had opened their own Teacher stores. In 1856 Teacher's opened the first dram store which not only sold whisky in bulk and in bottles for consumption off the premises, but whisky by the glass. This was the first of many innovations which William and his descendants were to introduce to the world of whisky.

William died in 1876 and his obituary in the Scottish Standard noted that, "Wherever Mr Teacher's name is known, and it is a household word in Scotland, . . . Success attended his efforts . . . Until by himself and by his sons, he held more shops in Glasgow, we believe, than any other firm connected with the Trade."

Teacher's started exporting in 1878 and their first order went to John Reid & Co Ltd in New Zealand. In 1884 the name Teacher's Highland Cream was registered by Robert Hart, who was the first non-family partner in the company.

In 1913 Teacher's launched the "Bury the Corkscrew" campaign. William Manera Bergius, William Teacher's grandson, had invented a new cork with a rim at the top, which could be removed simply by twisting it out of the bottle.

THE FAMOUS GROUSE

www.thefamousgrouse.co.uk

OWNERS: EDRINGTON GROUP

COMPANY FOUNDED: 1800

BLEND FIRST LAUNCHED: 1896

Matthew Gloag & Son was established as a grocer and wine merchant in Perth in 1800. For the next six generations, the company grew and through its association with leading distillers started to store stocks of fine whiskies. In 1896 Matthew Gloag created their first whisky and called it the "Grouse Brand." His daughter Phillipa drew the first label. This was quite an unusual step, as at the time brands were usually named after the founders. The red grouse is a game bird, which can still be found in the highlands of Scotland.

The blend quickly gained a reputation for quality and consistency and an 1897 advertisement shows the words "The Famous" added in handwriting to the brand. Several of the signature single malts found in a bottle of The Famous Grouse, such as The Macallan and Highland Park, now belong to the Edrington Group.

For years the company occupied a prime position in Perth at Bordeaux House, Kinoull Street. There were cellars with fine wines, a magnificent panelled boardroom, and reception area. I well remember visiting there and meeting some very special people, such as the late Alec Sherriff, who nurtured my interest in whisky.

The Famous Grouse spends several months marrying in Sherry casks after blending.

If you want to know more about The Famous Grouse visit the Glenturret Distillery near Crieff.

There are two versions, The Famous Grouse Finest and The Famous Grouse 10 year old blended malt.

THE FAMOUS GROUSE FINEST 40% (80°)

Color   Warm gold.

Nose   Intense, dry, spicy grain, and oak.

Taste   Warm caramel malt and grain intermingle with spice and fruit, medium bodied satisfying finish.

WHYTE & MACKAY

www.whyteandmackay.com

OWNERS: WHYTE & MACKAY LIMITED

COMPANY FOUNDED: 1843

BLEND FIRST LAUNCHED: 1896

James Whyte and Charles Mackay worked for general merchants Allan & Poynter, which was founded in 1843 in Glasgow. By the time they joined the company in 1875 only William Scott remained of the original partners. When William Scott died, James and Charles were successful in purchasing the wine and spirit side of the business and the stores at 35, Ann Street, Glasgow. They were not able to keep the original name so they call their company Whyte & Mackay. In 1882 the business transferred to new warehouses in Robertson Lane.

They continued to operate as wine and spirit warehousemen and merchants until 1896 when they created their own blend. Whyte & Mackay opened offices in the Baltic Chamber at 50, Wellington Street. In 1897 the first issue of the *West Australian Sunday Times* had a front-page advertisement, "Drink Only Whyte & Mackay Whisky."

The company was incorporated in 1919 and John McIlraith who had joined the company straight from school became managing director. Charles Mackay died in 1919 and James Whyte in 1921, his son Hartley Waddington Whyte joined the board at the age of 23.

Whyte & Mackay owes a great deal to their Master Blender Richard Paterson who has been with the company since 1970. Whyte & Mackay blends are created by marrying the chosen single malts in Sherry butts for three months and then adding six different grain whiskies to the malts and returning everything to Sherry butts for further maturation until bottling.

WHYTE & MACKAY SPECIAL 40% (80°)

Color   Amber gold.

Nose   Light vanilla and a hint of sulfur smoke from the Sherry casks with raisins, hazelnuts, and a grain prickle.

Taste   The grain on the nose is there on the mouth with raisins and vanilla coming through wrapped around a spicy dryness.

WHYTE & MACKAY THE THIRTEEN
13 YEAR OLD 40% (80°)

Color   Warm copper gold with mahogany reflectance.

Nose   Apples and pears, vanilla, caramel fudge, oak, and sulfur Sherry notes.

Taste   An intensely flavored blend full of strong caramel, malted barley, kumquat, and spiced fruits.

WHYTE & MACKAY SUPREME 22 YEAR OLD
43% (86°)

Color   Warm amber with light mahogany.

Nose   Intense nose with vanilla, butterscotch, light spice, dried fruits.

Taste   Rich, fills the mouth with sherried caramel, plums, and raisins with a dry, honey spice finish.

www.grantswhisky.com

OWNERS: WILLIAM GRANT & SONS

COMPANY FOUNDED: 1886

BRAND FIRST LAUNCHED: 1890

In September 2001 I received an invitation to "William Grant's & Paul McKenna Exclusive Preview of some Unforgettable Finishes" to be held at Simon Drake's Victorian House of Magic in London; this was a venue with a difference. Paul McKenna, a celebrity hypnotist, hypnotised a couple of volunteers, but this was not the real reason for the invitation . . .

We were there to taste two new finished expressions of Grant's The Family Reserve blended whisky — Grant's Ale Cask Reserve and Grant's Sherry Cask Reserve. The story of William Grant and the whisky dynasty he created is told in the Glenfiddich section (page 56).

William Grant's The Family Reserve is a traditional blended whisky, a favorite with many connoisseurs, a subtle blend of single malts and grain whiskies packed with flavor.

Grant's Ale Cask Reserve combines the ale notes from Edinburgh Strong Ale, which is produced by the Caledonian Brewing Company. Linking the arts of brewing and distilling would appear to be incompatible, but using William Grant & Sons in-house skills an interesting Scotch whisky has been created.

WILLIAM GRANT'S THE FAMILY RESERVE 40% (80°)

Color   Light gold.

Nose   Well rounded, balanced nose, there's malt, a hint of smoke, stewed prunes, light honey, and oak.

Taste   The elements on the nose are all replicated in the mouth with the addition of a creaminess from the grain. A satisfying, yet changing finish.

GRANT'S ALE CASK RESERVE 40% (80°)

Color   Golden summer.

Nose   Light, fresh.

Taste   There's a lot going on in the mouth, a mixture of malt and caramel and fruit and a long finish with a little smokiness.

GRANT'S SHERRY CASK RESERVE 40% (80°)

Color   Deep gold.

Nose   Sweet, oak, vanillins, smoke.

Taste   A sweeter flavor with some wood dryness on the tongue — yet there is still a hint of smoke in the finish.

WILLIAM LAWSON'S

www.dewarsworldofwhisky.com

OWNERS: JOHN DEWAR & SONS/BACARDI

COMPANY FOUNDED: 1849

William Lawson, a Scotch whisky merchant based in Dundee, produced "Lawson's Liqueur Whisky" for E & J Burke (also trading as W Lawson & Co), blenders and bottlers, of Dublin in the nineteenth century. William registered the trademark himself as the company's export manager. He became director of the company but was fired by Burke's in 1903. Burke's continued to promote the name Lawson. Around 1923 the business moved from Dublin to Liverpool and exports of their whisky brands increased. A large proportion of sales were made to the United States through the Bahamas during Prohibition.

The brand was purchased by Martini & Rossi in 1963 and they grouped all their whisky interests together under the name William Lawson Distilleries. The brand name was changed from Lawson's to William Lawson at this time. The group became part of Bacardi in 1995.

At the heart of William Lawson's blended whiskies is Glen Deveron Single Malt from the Macduff Distillery. William Lawson purchased Macduff in 1972.

The flagship Lawson's brand is William Lawson's Finest Blended and this has been popular throughout Europe for over 50 years. Total sales each year are more than 1 million cases.

William Lawson's Scottish Gold was created in 1983. This is a blend of 12 year old malt and grain Scotch whiskies.

WILLIAM LAWSON'S FINEST BLENDED 40% (80°)

Color   Pale summer gold.

Nose   A complex nose with grain, spiced apples and vanilla.

Taste   Mellow grain on the nose appears in the mouth with spicy, sweet honeyed notes.

WILLIAM LAWSON'S SCOTTISH GOLD 40% (80°)

Color   Light summer gold.

Nose   Pear drops, acacia honey, grain punch, and malt background notes.

Taste   Warm honeyed with the smoothness of the grain and malt punch, lingering spicy comforting finish.

OTHER SCOTTISH BLENDS

A list of blended Scotch whiskies and blends from other whisky-producing countries around the world would probably fill several other books this size. There are thousands of different brand names. This list simply features a few blends which have been brought to my attention and for which I did not have space to show in more detail.

CHIVAS BROTHERS PERNOD RICARD

www.chivas.com

CLAN CAMPBELL

Clan Campbell, which is a leading blend in the French market, is available as a blend and as Clan Campbell Pure Malt 10 year old.

100 PIPERS

100 Pipers is one of the world's major blended Scotch whiskies, which sells in Thailand, Spain, Venezuela, Australia, and India among other countries. 100 Pipers is available as a blend and as 100 Pipers 8 year old blended malt whisky.

SOMETHING SPECIAL

Something Special is a leading blend in Venezuela and Colombia and was launched in 1912 by Hill Thompson & Co. Something Special is available as a blend and Something Special 15 year old.

PASSPORT

Sales of this whisky make it one of the top 20 Scotch whisky brands in Brazil, Spain, USA, Mexico, and Eastern Europe.

DIAGEO

www.diageo.com

BUCHANAN'S

James Buchanan founded his company in 1884 and was a pioneer in the art of blending. Buchanan's Deluxe blend has Dalwhinnie at its heart. Buchanan was also responsible for another famous brand Black & White, which is still marketed by Diageo.

DIMPLE

The Dimple bottle is instantly recognizable and was first created in 1893 by the Haig whisky family. The Haigs started producing whisky in 1627 and were responsible for many developments in the distilling and blending of whisky. Dimple is available as Dimple Deluxe Blend, 12, 15, and 18 years old.

OLD PARR

Thomas Parr was reputedly the oldest living man in England and a painting of him by Rubens is shown on bottles of Old Parr. Cragganmore is the key single malt in this blend. Old Parr is available as Grand Old Parr 12 year old, Old Parr 15 year old, and Old Parr Superior 18 year old.

WINDSOR

The world's best selling super premium Scotch whisky available at 12, 17, and 21 years old.

Diageo also markets other brands including **Spey Royal**, a blend of Speysides, **The Real MacKenzie**, **Haig**, and **White Horse**.

INVER HOUSE DISTILLERS

www.inverhouse.com

CATTO'S

Catto's was first produced by James Catto in 1861, a merchant trader in Aberdeen. The brand was purchased by Inver House in 1990 and uses 18 different single malts and 3 different grains to make up their signature blends. Catto's is available unaged and at 12 years old.

CATTO'S BLENDED SCOTCH WHISKY 40% (80°)

Color	Pale summer gold.
Nose	Sharp grain notes then warmer.
Taste	Fills the mouth with malt, honey, shortbread, and spice.

HANKEY BANNISTER

Hankey Bannister started in 1757 when the company opened as a wine and spirit merchants in the West End of London. The company quickly gained a reputation and their whiskies were favorites of many leading personalities including King George VI, King Edward VII, and Winston Churchill. Hankey Bannister is available unaged and at 12 and 21 years old and also as a blended malt.

HANKEY BANNISTER 21 YEAR OLD 43% (86°)

Color	Warm amber gold.
Nose	Spiced fruit, malted barley, caramel, and oak.
Taste	Complex well constructed with warm caramel and fruit, and a dry lingering finish.

MORRISON BOWMORE

www.morrisonbowmore.co.uk

PRIME BLUE

Prime Blue was created in 2004 by Morrison Bowmore for the Taiwanese and Korean markets. The range is available as Prime Blue Standard, Prime Blue 12, 17, and 21 years old. Prime Blue is a Blended Malt containing only single malt whiskies.

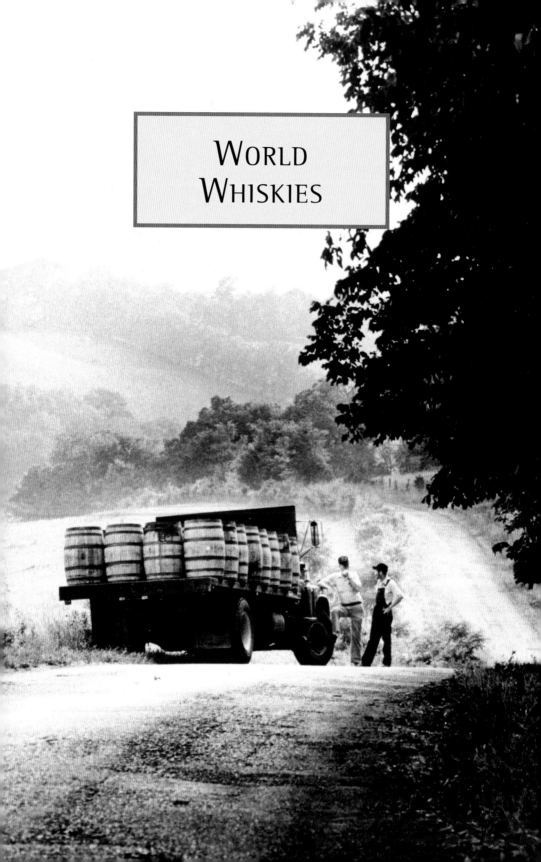

WORLD
WHISKIES

IRISH WHISKEYS

BUSHMILLS

NORTHERN IRELAND

COOLEY DISTILLERY
CONNEMARA
GREENORE
TYRCONNELL

KILBEGGAN

REPUBLIC OF IRELAND

MIDLETON

Ireland is for some the birthplace of whisky as we know it today. Whether whisky distilling started in Ireland or Scotland will probably never be known.

Irish whiskey is produced differently. Early whiskeys were made from a mixture of malted barley, malt, oats, wheat, and rye. By 1960, wheat, rye, and oats ceased to be used. Pot still whiskeys are currently made from a mix of malt and barley. By altering the percentages, different pot still whiskeys can be produced from light to heavy. The "weight" of a pot still whiskey can also be altered by allowing the middle cut spirit to run a little longer so that some of the heavier oils are captured.

Most Irish whiskey is triple distilled. The tradition of triple distilling in Ireland probably only dates from the end of Prohibition when the Irish sought to attract back the American drinkers by producing something lighter than traditional Scotch whiskies. Triple distillation takes place at Midleton and Bushmills, but not at Cooley where it is distilled only twice.

Midleton, like Cooley, also has Coffey or column stills for producing grain whiskey. At Midleton, grain whiskey is produced using principally maize, although some distillations are from a mix of malt and barley.

BUSHMILLS

Northern Ireland

Old Bushmills Distillery
Bushmills, Co Antrim BT57 8XH
Tel: +44 28 207 33218
www.bushmills.com

OWNERS: DIAGEO

FOUNDED: 1784

VISITOR CENTER: YES

Bushmills' history is inextricably linked with that of Irish distilling. There are stories of distilling as early as 1276 in the area and certainly by the 1600s there were many mills with distilleries along the River Bush.

Distilling reputedly started on the Bushmills site in 1608. On April 20, 1608 the Crown granted the monopoly to distil spirits "within the county of Colrane . . . or within the territory called the Rowte in County Antrim" to Sir Thomas Phillips, the governor of Ulster. The Rowte area lies between the Bush and Bann rivers, where Bushmills is situated. Bushmills, however, was not licensed until 1784, so it is not the oldest licensed distillery in Ireland. That accolade belongs to Kilbeggan, although it is certainly true that Bushmills has been almost continuously open (apart from a fire in 1885), whereas Kilbeggan has been silent for some time.

The 1850 Malt Tax increased the cost of malted barley in Ireland. As a result most of the Irish distillers started using a mixture of malted and unmalted barley in their production to save money. Bushmills did not however change its style and continued using 100% malted barley.

Bushmills single malt whiskey is triple-distilled. The Bushmills family also includes blended whiskies. Bushmills Original is a blend of triple-distilled Bushmills malt whiskey with a lighter Irish grain whiskey. Black Bush is a special blend with a high proportion of the malt matured in Oloroso Sherry casks.

BUSHMILLS 10 YEAR OLD 40% (80°)

Color   Summer gold.

Nose   The mixture of Bourbon and former Oloroso Sherry casks adds warm honey, Sherry, and spice to the nose.

Taste   Warm, smooth with full flavors of sweetness, spice, malted barley, and a hint of chocolate.

Bushmills Malt is available at 10, 16, and 21 years old.

CONNEMARA

Ireland

Cooley Distillery
Cooley, Co Louth
Tel: +353 42937 6102
www.connemarawhiskey.com

OWNERS: COOLEY DISTILLERY PLC

FOUNDED: 1987

VISITOR CENTER: NO

Cooley is really older than 1987, but this story begins here because in 1987 John Teeling bought the distillery. Cooley or Ceimici Teo was a state-owned Irish alcohol distillery which closed in 1986. John's dream to revive old brands such as Tyrconnell and Lockes attracted other investors, such as Willie McCarter who owned part of the old Watts Distillery, Paul Power, and Lee Mallaghan, who owned Locke's Distillery.

At Cooley Distillery there are two pot stills, which are used to create malt whiskies using 100% malted Irish barley. There is also a patent still, which makes grain whiskey from a mixture of malted barley and maize. The grain whiskey is used in the company's blends and also to create Greenore (see page 112).

Connemara Peated Single Malt Irish Whiskey is made at Cooley using local peat to dry the barley after malting, which was common in the past. The company has revived this ancient tradition to create "a whiskey to make the illicit distillers of the past proud." Connemara is a well-known mountainous region of Ireland and the distillery gets its water from a reservoir in the Cooley Mountains. Connemara is matured in ex-Bourbon barrels at the Lockes Distillery in Kilbeggan, Co Westmeath.

Connemara is available unaged at 40% (80°) and Connemara cask strength, and Connemara 12 year old.

CONNEMARA PEATED SINGLE MALT IRISH WHISKEY 12 YEAR OLD 40% (80°)

Color   Pale gold with a slight greenish tinge.

Nose   Strong smoky nose with a hint of bramble hedges, honeysuckle, and wet leaves.

Taste   Surprisingly, the strength of the peat is initially mellowed by a warm sweetness from the hedgerow themes encountered on the nose. Then the full impact of the smokiness comes through. With a long, smooth aftertaste.

CONNEMARA CASK STRENGTH PEATED SINGLE MALT IRISH WHISKEY 58.8% (117.6°)

Color   Pale gold.

Nose   The nose is innocently mild at first, with hints of toffee, then peat smoke, and an unexpected element of the sea.

Taste   The mouthfeel is oily and the flavors are gloriously full and harmonious. The sweetness of the malt combines with the strength of peat smoke and sea salt. A big finish with sweetness and smoke gradually dying away to a light dryness.

GREENORE

Ireland

Cooley Distillery
Cooley, Co Louth
Tel: +353 42937 6102
www.cooleywhiskey.com

OWNERS: COOLEY DISTILLERY PLC

FOUNDED: 1987

VISITOR CENTER: No

Greenore is the oldest single grain Irish whiskey. Single grain whiskies are the backbone of the distilling industry worldwide and they constitute between 40% and 60% of the content of a blend. The balance of a blend in Scotland is made from single malt whiskies and in Ireland from different whiskeys as described elsewhere in this section. Bottlings of single grain whiskies are therefore relatively rare.

Greenore is made at Cooley Distillery, which was an old Irish alcohol plant built to a high standard. The Coffey still's plates are made from perforated copper, which creates a cleaner spirit and a fine grain whiskey.

Greenore whiskey is made using soft water from the Cooley Mountains and grain to create a light, aromatic whiskey, which is full of flavor. Greenore is matured in Bourbon oak casks at the company's Kilbeggan distillery in the 200-year-old warehouses.

The current bottling is an 8 year old limited to 5,000 bottles and new releases are forecast at 10, 16, and 18 years old.

GREENORE SINGLE GRAIN 8 YEAR OLD 40% (80°)

Color   Warm summer gold.

Nose   A really light whiskey with a delicately perfumed aroma of flowers and ripe grain. The nose expands to reflect the Bourbon oak casks with vanilla and green wood notes.

Taste   The delicate flowery elements unfold to a round richness, which fills the mouth with a hint of cinnamon, allspice, fruit, and barley. A sweetness lingers on the tongue but there is a surprise in the finish, which is dry and spicy.

JAMESON

Ireland

The Old Jameson Distillery
Bow Street, Smithfield, Dublin 7
Tel: +353 1807 2355
www.irishdistillers.ie / www.jamesonwhiskey.com

OWNERS: IRISH DISTILLERS/ PERNOD RICARD

FOUNDED: 1780

VISITOR CENTER: YES

John Jameson founded his distillery in 1780 in the heart of Dublin. The distillery history is that Jameson came to Ireland from Scotland with his wife who was a member of the Scottish Haig family. They had two sons, John Junior and William. John Junior took over the Dublin distillery, while his brother William worked at Marrowbone Lane distillery with John Stein. Jameson was one of the first to use Sherry casks for maturing his whiskeys.

By the late 1800s the Jameson brothers owned both distilleries and became the biggest Irish distiller. By 1880, 300 people were employed and the company was producing 1.2 million gallons of whiskey annually. The stills were huge — the wash still had a capacity of 28,824 gallons and the two low wines 16,800 and 15,600 gallons. These large stills were similar to those used at the time in the Lowlands of Scotland, and the effect of the huge fires underneath was to "cook" the spirit.

Most sales were made in the cask, bottling did not start until 1968. Before then casks were sold to companies who bottled the contents under their own brand names. Crested Ten and Red Seal were the first brands to be bottled by Jameson's.

Jameson is no longer made in Dublin, but at the company's Midleton distillery. Jameson is a blend of Irish malt, pot still, and grain whiskeys.

Jameson is the best known Irish whiskey and some 1.5 million glasses are drunk every day. Current Jameson bottlings are Jameson no age, Jameson 12 year old, and Jameson 18 year old.

JAMESON 40% (80°)

Color	Light gold.
Nose	Clean fresh grain notes with the sharper notes of Sherry, intense malt, and dark caramel.
Taste	Full bodied fills the mouth with vanilla, caramel, and dried fruit.

KILBEGGAN

Ireland

Locke's Distillery
Kilbeggan, Co Westmeath
Tel: +353 506 32134
www.cooleywhiskey.com

OWNERS: COOLEY DISTILLERY PLC

FOUNDED: 1757

VISITOR CENTER: YES

Kilbeggan is Gaelic for "Little Church" and is the site of the distillery started by John Locke in 1757 on the banks of the River Brusna. Kilbeggan or Locke's distillery can claim to be the world's oldest continually licensed distillery. From the records for the Trim excise district there were 43 stills in the district in 1766.

The distillery's fortunes changed a great deal during the next 200 years. John Locke's son, John, ran the distillery from the mid-nineteenth century. His wife, Mary Anne, took over in 1868 and ran the distillery with the manager Walter Furlong until 1880 when her eldest son John was old enough to take over at the age of 26. During Mary Anne's tenure the distillery was well run and sales increased around the world and to the growing English market.

John and his younger brother James initially ran the distillery well, but in the long term sales declined. In 1901 fire broke out but because funds were tight repairs weren't carried out till 1918. Then in 1920 Prohibition was introduced in the United States, a market which was just opening up for Locke's. John Edward died in 1920 and James Harvey in 1927 at one of the worst times in the distillery's history. The glory days were never to return and after the depressions, two World Wars, and a scandal, the distillery closed in 1958.

On March 19, 2007 Kilbeggan woke again and the refurbished old pot still was fired 53 years to the day when distilling stopped in 1954.

KILBEGGAN IRISH WHISKEY 40% (80°)

Color   Warm gold.

Nose   Sweet malted barley, a complex nose with hints of sweet corn and hops.

Taste   The complexity of the nose is reflected in the mouth. The overall taste is malty with elements of a lightly spiced Christmas cake with sultanas, currants, cinnamon, and honey. A short dry slightly spicy finish.

MIDLETON

Ireland

Midleton Distillery
The Old Distillery, Midleton, Co Cork
Tel: +353 21 461 3594
www.irishdistillers.ie

OWNERS: IRISH DISTILLERS/ PERNOD RICARD

FOUNDED: 1796

VISITOR CENTER: YES

Visiting whisky distilleries is always a pleasure and often they are built in beautiful parts of the world. The city of Cork is a superb tourist destination built on a number of hills with small backstreets and fine buildings. Cork has some different places to visit such as the Butter Museum, for much of its wealth was created through the sale of butter, and the Beamish and Murphy Breweries.

While there you must kiss the Blarney Stone, which traditionally makes you very talkative or gives you "the gift of the gab." Distilleries like North Mall or The Watercourse, which were located in Cork are long gone. To find the nearest distillery you will have to drive into the countryside to Midleton and the former James Murphy distillery.

The modern distillery, which is built alongside the old one, was completed in 1975. There are still bottlings to be found of whiskeys produced at the old distillery, but clearly they won't be around for long!

Midleton is now the only working distillery belonging to Irish Distillers, part of Pernod-Ricard in Ireland. Midleton produces all three types of Irish whiskeys, pot still, malt, and grain. Pot still whiskey is made from both malt and unmalted barley. Malt whiskey is, as elsewhere, made from malted barley. Grain whiskey is made in a continuous still from maize, wheat, and some barley.

Midleton is bottled as a pot still whiskey and matured in ex-Bourbon casks for 12 to 25 years. Midleton Very Rare was launched in 1984 and "vintages" are released each year.

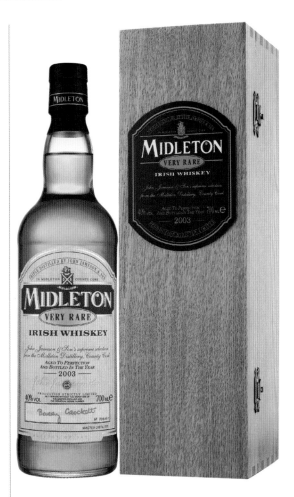

MIDLETON VERY RARE
(Distillery tasting notes.)

Color   Mid gold.

Nose   Spicy bouquet with floral and herbal touches.

Taste   Scented pot still whiskey with almonds, lush fruits, and honey mixed with herbal spice. Velvety smooth, long finish.

TYRCONNELL

Ireland

Cooley Distillery
Cooley, Co Louth
Tel: +353 42937 6102
www.tyrconnellwhiskey.com

OWNERS: COOLEY DISTILLERY PLC

BRAND FIRST LAUNCHED AROUND 1839

VISITOR CENTER: No

Tyrconnell distillery dates from around 1839 when wine and spirit merchant Andrew Watt took over the Waterside Distillery, Abbey Street, Derry in Northern Ireland. It is believed that a distillery had been on the same site since 1762. A Coffey still was installed with assistance from Aeneas Coffey and from then on the success of the distillery was assured. Soon it was producing 2 million gallons (9 million liters) of whiskey annually and much of this was being sold in the United States. The company was also exporting to England, Canada, Australia, and Nigeria.

In 1902 four distilleries, the Connswater, Avoniel, Abbey, and Waterside Distilleries linked together to form United Distilleries Ltd. A price war between UDC and the Scottish Distillers Company resulted in the two companies amalgamating.

The 1914 edition of Harper's Directory lists, "Watt, David, & Co. Ltd., Distillers and Yeast Manufacturers, Londonderry, Distillers of Grain Whiskey, at Abbey Street Distillery, and of Pot-Still whiskey at Waterside Distillery. Established about 100 years ago, and incorporated in 1888."

However, the advent of Prohibition and problems between UDC and Scottish Distillers Company meant that by 1925 the distillery closed.

Tyrconnell was relaunched with the creation of Cooley Distillery plc in 1987 by John Teeling and, among others, Willie McCarter who owned part of the old Watts Distillery. Tyrconnell is a recreation of an original Irish single malt whiskey without any peat influences.

TYRCONNELL SINGLE MALT IRISH WHISKEY 40% (80°)

Color   Warm golden yellow.

Nose   First notes are summery with fresh mown hay, a hint of lemons and oranges, and a breath of heather. This lightness is backed by real malt warmth and a hint of spice.

Taste   The sweetness on the nose is the first to come through on the tongue. A round, well balanced whiskey with citrus, malt, honey, and an oily mouthfeel. A long complex finish with malted barley and a hint of sweetness.

OTHER IRISH WHISKEYS

Irish whiskeys that are produced as pure or single malts are listed elsewhere in this chapter.

This chapter has featured a couple of key Irish pot still and blended whiskeys; some more are shown below. This is not a definitive list; you will discover other blends.

COOLEY DISTILLERY PLC

www.cooleywhiskey.com

INISHOWEN IRISH WHISKEY 40% (80°)

Inishowen is the name of the most northern tip of Ireland, which is guarded by Burt Castle, the medieval home of the O'Doherty Clan. Inishowen is a peated, blended Irish whiskey.

Color   Medium light gold.

Nose   Peat then warm-scented garden with roses and fruit.

Taste   A lot going on in the mouth. First impressions are dry with warm flashes of sweetness and malted barley and then creamy grain and finally the smokiness of the peat comes through. Essentially dry with a hint of warmth in the finish.

LOCKE'S BLENDED IRISH WHISKEY & LOCKE'S 8 YEAR OLD SINGLE MALT

This famous brand was resurrected by Cooley Distillery in 1992. John Locke owned Kilbeggan Distillery from the mid-nineteenth century. The distillery was founded in 1757 in a former monastery. John Locke turned the business into an international name, exporting whiskey to Australia, Argentina, the United States, and the UK. More about the story of Locke's distillery can be found under Kilbeggan (page 114). Locke's whiskeys are currently produced at Cooley Distillery, but with the re-launch of Kilbeggan on the March 19, 2007, we may see Locke's single malt from its birthplace once again.

MILLARS SPECIAL RESERVE

In 1843 Adam Millar & Co wine, tea, and spirits merchants were founded in Dublin with offices close to St. Patrick's Cathedral. The company created its own Irish whiskey and for a time they also sold their own Scotch blend, Glenmillar. Their best selling brand was Millars Black Label, but to avoid confusion with Johnnie Walker Black Label when exporting overseas, the name was changed.

IRISH DISTILLERS

www.irishdistillers.ie

PADDY OLD IRISH WHISKEY 40% (80°)

You will see Paddy on almost any bar in Ireland and that is just the way that the Cork Distilleries' salesman Paddy Flaherty would have wished. In 1881 he joined the company and did much of his round on a bicycle. He soon established a reputation as a generous host and the publicans started asking for Paddy's Whiskey. The owners weren't best pleased but in the end the name of the brand was changed to Paddy. Paddy is a blended Irish whiskey.

Color   Mid-gold.

Nose   A light, warm malty aroma.

Taste   Light on the tongue with hints of malt and toasted hazelnuts and a soft finish.

POWERS

James Power stared his distillery in Dublin in 1791. His son John was the first whiskey distiller to produce a miniature bottle known as the "Baby Powers." Before the company could sell the new bottle an Act of Parliament had to be passed. Power's John Lane Distillery closed and the brand continues to be produced by Irish Distillers.

REDBREAST PURE POT STILL WHISKEY

Redbreast was the brand name given to pot still whiskey supplied by Jameson to his customers from 1939. The name almost disappeared following the start of bottling at the distillery; casks were no longer sold to independent bottlers. In 1990 the Redbreast name was re-launched by Irish Distillers. Redbreast is matured for at least 12 years in a mix of Sherry butts and Bourbon casks.

JAPANESE WHISKIES

Japanese whisky owes much of its origins to Scotland. The first distiller, Masataka Taketsuru, was trained in Scotland and brought back his newfound knowledge to traditional sake distilleries in Japan.

The landscape of the northern island, Hokkaido, is very similar to that of the highlands of Scotland, with peat bogs, mountains, and cool, fresh streams flowing over granite rocks. However, most of the Japanese distillers are not on Hokkaido but on the main island of Honshu. The Japanese have been distilling whisky since 1923 and production includes both single malts and blends. Only a few Japanese whiskies are sold as single malt, the majority are sold as blends. Most Japanese whisky is produced for the home market with about 3 percent exported principally to the Pacific. The two key players are Suntory and Nikka who are featured in this section. Hanyu, Shirakawa, and Mars Shinshu are currently closed although some whiskies are still available. Specialty whisky stores around the world stock some of the key brands highlighted in the following pages.

HAKUSHU

Japan

Hakushu Ditillery and Hakushu Higashi Distillery
Torihara 2913-1, Hakushu-machi, Hokuto, Yamanashi 408-0316
Tel: +81 551 35 2211
www.suntory.com

OWNERS: SUNTORY	
FOUNDED: 1973	
VISITOR CENTER: YES	

Hakushu distillery is located in Yamanashi Prefecture, which is to the west of Tokyo in the Chubu region. This is an area of outstanding beauty and the northern half of Mount Fuji and the Fuji Five Lake region are located in Yamanashi. This is a forested part of Japan with mountains, rushing streams, and an abundance of wildlife.

Hakushu distillery was built to coincide with the 50th anniversary of Yamazaki by Keizo Saji, Shinjiro Torii's second son. Shinjiro Torii founded Suntory in 1899. On completion, Hakushu was the world's biggest distillery. The company's publicity includes a picture of a kingfisher and there is a bird sanctuary at the distillery. Hakushu means "white sand bank" reflecting the color of the river bed. The company also bottles spring water here. The distillery is 2,300 feet (700 meters) above sea level, which is twice as high as Braeval. Because of its high altitude, distillation is at a lower pressure and this creates a lighter whisky.

Hakushu, like Yamazaki, is matured in a mix of ex-Bourbon casks, Sherry butts, and used Japanese water oak (Mizumara) barrels.

Hakushu Single Malt is available at 10, 12, and 18 years old.

HAKUSHU 10 YEAR OLD 40% (80°)

Color   Warm summer gold.

Nose   Initial notes are honey, vanilla, and barley then the smoke starts to come through.

Taste   Peat bonfires, spice with warm caramel and malt, with a dry smoke finish.

HAKUSHU 12 YEAR OLD 43.5% (87°)

Color   Warm summer gold.

Nose   Caramelized oranges with hints of licorice and smoke. With water the smoke aromas expand.

Taste   At first warm caramel with licorice, ripe fruit flavors, and big waves of smoke with a dry finish, with smoke and caramel lingering in the mouth.

HIBIKI

www.suntory.com

OWNERS: SUNTORY

BRAND FIRST LAUNCHED: 1989

VISITOR CENTER: NO

Suntory was established in 1899 as a food and beverage company at a time when whisky, gin, vodka, and other Western drinks were not readily available in Japan. The founder, Shinjiro Torii wanted to change all that and said, "I want to make whisky in Japan, whisky of the Japanese taste that will be enjoyed throughout the world." He achieved his dream and many of Suntory's whiskies are today enjoyed globally.

The company opened a chain of bars in Japan, "Tory's Bars," where whisky and other Western spirits were sold. A magazine *Youshu Tengoku* (Western Liquor Heaven) introduced readers to the new drinks.

In my book, *Whisky, Uisge Beatha: The Water of Life*, I featured some of Suntory's advertising. A 1960s advertisement showed a sweepstake offering the chance to visit Hawaii. The headline read, "Drink Torys Whisky . . . Go Hawaii," and this would have appealed to the Japanese who at that time rarely traveled abroad. Today whisky is very much a part of the Japanese way of life and customers can enjoy a wide variety of whiskies from home and overseas distillers. Kakubin is the company's oldest blend and other notable brands include The Old and Royal.

Hibiki is Suntory's premium blended whisky brand. Hibiki is a blend of grain and single malt whiskies. Hibiki is available at 17, 21, and 30 years old in striking ridged glass bottles with ornate stoppers and hand made paper labels.

HIBIKI 17 YEAR OLD 43% (86°)

Color   Light copper with red flashes.

Nose   Oak, peat, saddle leather. With water opens up to include malt, vanilla, and dried figs.

Taste   Warm, burned caramel, syrupy mouthfeel with malt undertones and a dry, licorice finish which lingers and becomes sweeter.

HIBIKI 21 YEAR OLD 43% (86°)

Color   Warm copper gold.

Nose   Molasses, sweet candied fruit, vanilla.

Taste   Syrup, burned sugar, spice with a dry finish.

NIKKA

Japan

Nikka Sendai Miyagikyo Distillery
Miyagiken Sendaishi, Aoba, Nikka-1
Tel: +81 22 395 2111
www.nikka.com

OWNERS: NIKKA

FOUNDED: 1969

VISITOR CENTER: YES

Japanese whisky owes much of its origins to Scotland and to one man in particular, Masataka Taketsuru. For more of his story, see the information on the Yoichi Distillery (page 123). He founded the Sendai (Miyagikyo) Distillery in 1969. Sendai is situated in the north of Japan's largest island, Honshu. Yoichi distillery is on Hokkaido, Japan's most northerly island. The site chosen by Masataka sits in the center of a mountainous region on a stretch of land between two rivers. With a ready supply of clean water the site seemed an ideal position for his new distillery, which produces a light single malt.

Sendai Distillery produces whisky using both conventional pot stills to create single malt whiskies and a Coffey or grain still. All Malt is a version made with whisky taken from the wash stills and then passed through the Coffey still. This is aged in oak casks and then mixed with standard single malt whisky. The result is a smoother, less expensive malt whisky.

There are a large number of bottlings from the Sendai Distillery. Some of them are labeled Miyagikyo (or Miyagikyou), others Sendai. Additionally, there are the Blended Malts such as All Malt described above, Nikka Malt 100 The Anniversary Aged 12 Years, Pure Malt White, which is a peated whisky, and expressions bearing the founder's name such as Taketsuru Pure Malt 21 year old.

SENDAI 12 YEAR OLD 45% (90°)
(Tasting notes from Nikka Chief Blender.)

Color   Deep gold.

Nose   Light touch of malt and floral note. Rich fruitiness and a hint of herb. Clean. Slightly prickles.

Taste   Light, balanced rich fruitiness with a hint of pear and malty sweetness. Refreshing acidity. Well balanced with gentle peat. Dry and light, smooth finish.

NIKKA PURE MALT WHITE 43% (86°)
(Tasted by the author at Daniel Le Maître's daughter's wedding in France.)

Color   Warm gold.

Nose   Sweet malty with light smoke overtones. With a little water, the peat smoke expands.

Taste   Full-bodied peat smoke, malt with hints of citrus and salt – long smoke-filled finish with honey back notes.

YAMAZAKI

Japan

Yamazaki Distillery
Yamazaki 5-2-1, Shimamoto-cho, Mishima-gun, Osaka 618-0001
Tel: +81 75 961 1234
www.suntory.com

OWNERS: SUNTORY

FOUNDED: 1923

VISITOR CENTER: YES

Yamazaki distillery was built by Shinjiro Torii with Masataka Taketsuru. Masataka had learned about the production of Scotch whisky at Bo'ness Grain and Hazelburn Campbeltown distilleries in Scotland. Suntory was founded in 1899 as a liquor and food business. Today, the company has diversified into pharmaceuticals, health foods, and flowers. If you are a gardener you may well have planted Surfinia petunias, which were cultivated by the company. There are Suntory companies around the world including Bowmore, Auchentoshan, and Glen Garioch distilleries in Scotland.

Yamazaki valley was originally named "Minaseno" which means source of water. The Imperial family used to visit the valley in the tenth century because of its clean, natural environment. The first whisky produced was Suntory Shirofuda in 1929 and this is still available as Suntory White. In 1937 Kakubin was launched and this still the leading brand in Japan and was featured in the film *Lost in Translation* with Bill Murray.

I attended a special launch of Yamazaki 18 year old on July 8, 2004 in the company of Dr. Kouichi Inatomi, Master Blender, who retired in 1999. He said he felt a bit like "the return of an old soldier and that after five years my knowledge of the company is thinning a little rather like my hair." We soon discovered that this was far from the truth. He said that when he started with the company over 40 years before, the average Japanese salary was £50, equivalent to the cost at that time of a bottle of Johnnie Walker Black Label.

YAMAZAKI 12 YEAR OLD 43% (86º)

(Matured in ex-Bourbon barrels, Sherry casks, and used Mizumara (Japanese water oak) barrels.

Color   Warm gold.

Nose   Light buttery sweetness, vanilla, sultanas, with pepper and wet wood undertones.

Taste   Undiluted strong malt notes. With water, stronger heavier elements come through, with iron filings, spice, and honey. Dry finish with a hint of spice and cream.

YAMAZAKI 18 YEAR OLD 43% (86º)

(Casks used are as above. The extra six years maturation has added maturity and depth of flavor to the single malt.)

Color   Warm dark gold with copper glints.

Nose   First notes are sulfur from the Sherry casks, but this is quickly taken over by apple and cinnamon crumble with currants and sultanas. With water the nose opens up to be creamier and sweeter.

Taste   Mouth coating sooty dryness with toasted hazelnuts and almonds, with warmer fruit notes such as cherry. The creaminess and sweetness found on the nose with water is replicated in the mouth with more fruit and sugar candy. A short finish with spiced fruit.

YOICHI

Japan

Nikka Yoichi Distillery,
Hokkaido Yoichigun Yoichimachi, Kurokawacho 7–6
Tel: +81 135 233131
www.nikka.com

OWNERS: NIKKA

FOUNDED: 1934

VISITOR CENTER: YES

Japanese whisky owes much of its origins to Scotland and to one man in particular, Masataka Taketsuru. Masataka was born in 1894 at Takehara near Hiroshima. The family owned a sake brewery, which was founded in 1773 and is still in production today. Masataka studied chemistry at university and went to Glasgow in Scotland to learn more about the brewing and distilling business. He worked at Hazelburn and Bo'ness distilleries and studied at Glasgow University. Masataka returned to Japan in 1921 with his Scottish wife Jessie who he had married the year before.

On his return, he learned that in the meantime the family business had decided not to produce different Western style spirits, so he joined Suntory. (See Yamazaki, opposite, for the story of this distillery.)

After 10 years with Suntory, which included trips to France and Great Britain studying whisky and wine production, Masataka left to found his own distillery. From his experience in Scotland, he knew that finding the right site was important and explored the north island of Japan, Hokkaido, where there are mountains, a steady supply of pure water, and peat bogs.

In 1934 he established the Danipponkaju Company and built Yoichi distillery. In 1952 the company changed its name to the Nikka Whisky Distilling Co Ltd. Masataka died in 1979 at the age of 85, having received many honors from his country and established a thriving, dynamic whisky industry in Japan.

YOICHI 10 YEAR OLD 43% (86°)
(Tasting notes from Nikka Master Blender)

Color Deep gold.

Nose Fruity, sweet, malty, vanilla, pleasant peat.

Taste Medium bodied, good balanced sweetness from malt with aged wood. Ripe fruits, smoothness, cinnamon. Heavy but not so long, fragrant, lingering, refreshing finish.

YOICHI 12 YEAR OLD 43% (86°)
(Tasting notes from Nikka Master Blender)

Color Amber.

Nose Woody, gently peaty, nutty. Dried fruits. Aromatic.

Taste Medium to full body. Sweet and smooth. Firm oak. Well balanced with gentle peat. Lingering oak flavor and pleasant peat finish.

YOICHI 15 YEAR OLD 45% (90°)

Color Deep amber-red.

Nose Complex flavor comes from fermentation and aged wood. Orange, tropical fruits, oily nuts with massive peat.

Taste Full bodied. Nuts, leather, slight hint of sulfur, ripe fruits, robustness and complexity. A well aged regal whisky. Long smoky, oily, very complex finish.

USA AND CANADIAN WHISKEYS

The first Puritan settlers did not bring whisky to America. It was not until immigrants from Scotland and Ireland arrived that production started and spread westward. Pennsylvania, Maryland, and Virginia became the key whiskey producing areas. It is ironic to learn that George Washington, who was responsible for quelling the Whiskey Rebellion (mentioned in the introductory pages), was himself a distiller.

Bourbons date from the 1700s, although very few companies have distilled continuously. Jim Beam was founded in the early 1800s. Bourbons are essentially created in the same way as Single Malts as described in the first chapters of this book. There are differences, one being the sour mash method, which means that a little of the mash is kept back and added to the next batch of grains during cooking or mashing.

Elijah Craig is credited with introducing the charring of barrels inside to produce the distinctive Bourbon taste, following a fire in his cask warehouse. Other differences are mentioned under the appropriate brands.

American and Canandian whiskey production suffered as a result of Prohibition and has never returned to those glorious days, so often typified in the movies.

American whiskeys are predominantly Bourbon with some Tennessee, including the giant Jack Daniel's. There are some corn whiskeys, straight ryes, and more recently a few single malts being produced.

ANCHOR DISTILLING CO

USA

Anchor Brewing Company
1705 Mariposa Street, San Francisco, CA 94107
Tel: +1 415 863 8350
www.anchorbrewing.com

OWNERS: ANCHOR DISTILLING CO/FRITZ MAYTAG

FOUNDED: 1993

VISITOR CENTER: YES

The Anchor Brewing Company was founded in 1896 by Ernst F. Baruth and his son-in-law Otto Schinkel, who purchased an existing distillery, founded in the 1850s by Gottlieb Brekle. The company brews many beers including their famous Anchor Steam Beer. In 1993 the Anchor Distilling Co was launched by Fritz Meytag to recreate small batch whiskeys and other distilled spirits such as Junipero gin. The whiskeys are marketed under the brand name of Old Potrero and bottlings are made from 100% malted rye.

There is Old Potrero's Hotaling's Whiskey which commemorates the 1906 San Francisco earthquake when 4.7 square miles (12.1 square kilometers) were subsequently devastated by fire and explosions including 28,188 buildings and many churches. Thousands of people also lost their lives. The clergy felt that the earthquake was retribution for the high living enjoyed by many natives of San Francisco. Walking back from the fire, Professor Jerome Baker Landfield was with Charles Kellogg Field who penned the following poem, "If as they say God sparked the town, For being over frisky, Why did He burn the churches down, And Save Hotaling's Whiskey." Apparently thousands of barrels of Hotaling's whiskey survived the fire.

Other bottlings including Old Potrero Single Malt Rye Whiskey 19th Century Style and Old Potrero Single Malt Rye Whiskey 18th Century Style.

**OLD POTRERO SINGLE MALT HOTALINGS
11 YEAR OLD 50% (100°)**

Color   Warm gold.

Nose   Amazing mixture of rye, orange, caramel, all spice, and dark chocolate.

Taste   Rye predominates although much of the aromas on the nose are reflected in the taste with vanilla. A light finish.

BUFFALO TRACE

USA

Buffalo Trace Distillery
1001 Wilkinson Boulevard, Franklin County, KY 40601
Tel: +1 502 696 5926
www.buffalotrace.com

OWNERS: BUFFALO TRACE DISTILLERY INC

FOUNDED: 1787

VISITOR CENTER: YES

Before settlers first came to this part of the United States, buffalo crossed the land following set paths, which were known as traces. The Great Buffalo Trace was the route taken by Daniel Boone and George Rogers Clark to a fertile area close to the Kentucky River. It is here that Buffalo Trace was born and it is believed distilling started on the site in 1787. The first steam-powered distillery was built in 1857 and later purchased by E. J. Taylor, Jr. who was responsible for enhancing the production of Kentucky Bourbon overall and improving the warehousing facilities at Buffalo Trace.

Buffalo Trace was one of only four distilleries to continue making spirit for medicinal purposes during the Prohibition era. After Prohibition the distillery passed to Albert Blanton who started producing single-barrel Bourbon for close friends and family. In 1984 the company was the first to promote single-barrel Bourbons and this continues to this day with some very special bottlings.

Each bottling of Buffalo Trace is created from 35 barrels, which are personally selected by the master distiller. Buffalo Trace prides itself on its purity and the naturalness of its products. At the distillery you will see a sign which says "No chemists allowed" – I think this says it all.

As a little aside it is interesting to note that Buffalo Trace is the only Kentucky distillery producing vodka.

BUFFALO TRACE 45% (90°)

Color   Bright coppery gold.

Nose   This whiskey packs a punch initially and then lighter hints of vanilla, burned caramel, and mint come through.

Taste   Honey sweetness on the tongue with lots of vanilla oak, licorice, and hints of dark chocolate.

BULLEIT BOURBON

USA

Bulleit Distilling Company
Lawrenceburg, KY 40342
Tel: +1 859 229 5171
www.bulleitbourbon.com

OWNERS: DIAGEO

BRAND FIRST LAUNCHED: 1830

VISITOR CENTER: NO

Bulleit Bourbon has its origins in New Orleans, for it is here that the Bulleit family arrived from France in the 1700s. Augustus Bulleit moved to Louisville, Kentucky in 1830 and began producing Bourbon to his own recipe. It should be remembered that at that time, Bourbon would have been distilled in small batches, a style which has been resurrected by many distillers today.

Augustus had arrived in Kentucky at the right period in America's history. Frontiersmen traveled through Kentucky as they headed west and the fame of Bulleit Bourbon went with them. Sadly, this was to be shortlived as in 1860 Augustus was traveling from Kentucky to New Orleans with a load of barrels and died on the way. The Bulleit Bourbon distillery died with him.

But, like all good stories, this was not the end of Bulleit Bourbon. Tales of this unique whiskey were passed from father to son and the family dreamed of resurrecting the brand. In 1987, over 100 years since Augustus died, Tom Bulleit finally revived the brand using the original recipe. Bulleit is created with a minimum of 51% corn, but has a higher rye content, which gives the whiskey its distinctive taste and aroma. Bulleit whiskey is placed in American white oak barrels and stored in a traditional single-story warehouse. This ensures that all whiskey matures at the same rate, producing a consistent style.

The Bulleit bottle is oval in shape, similar to those used during the middle of the 1800s.

BULLEIT BOURBON KENTUCKY STRAIGHT BOURBON WHISKEY 45% (90°)

Color   Copper gold.

Nose   The first notes are filled with rye and burned caramel, then honey and oak.

Taste   In the mouth full bodied, rich grain and caramel sweetness with a dry, roasted nuts, yet with hints of sugary popcorn, medium finish.

CANADIAN CLUB

Canada

Canadian Club Brand Heritage Center
2072 Riverside Drive East, Walkerville, Ontario N8Y 4S5
Tel: +1 519 973 9503
www.canadianclubwhisky.com

OWNERS: BEAM GLOBAL SPIRITS & WINE

BLEND FIRST LAUNCHED: 1858

VISITOR CENTER: YES

Canadian Club was developed by one of the whisky industry's leading personalities in the nineteenth century – Hiram Walker. Hiram was born in 1816 and at the age of nine his father died. He left his home town of Douglas, Massachusetts and started working in a grocer's shop in Boston at the age of 20. In 1838 he moved to Detroit and by 1846 he had his own grocery and spirits store. The growth of the Temperance Movement which swept America changed his business and the State of Michigan no longer permitted the sale of alcohol. Undaunted, Hiram transferred his activities across the Detroit River into Canada. In 1858 he built the Windsor Distillery and Flouring Mill in Windsor, Ontario.

Most whisky at that time was sold in plain barrels, usually without a maker's name. Hiram decided to bottle his as Walker's Club Whisky and its fame soon spread, particularly across the border in America. As a result, he had to change the name to Canadian Club to differentiate it from American whiskeys.

The distilling and milling business expanded considerably and by 1870 built Walkerville – a vast site with maltings, a dairy farm, and housing. The two major contributions Hiram made to Canadian whisky were the creation of multiple column distillation and the art of blending.

Canadian Club is available at 6 years standard 40% (80°) and at 50% (100°), as Canadian Club Classic 12 year, Canadian Club Reserve, and Canadian Club Sherry Cask aged for a minimum of 8 years with secondary maturation in Sherry casks.

CANADIAN CLUB 40% (80°)

Color   Warm gold.

Nose   An intense nose strong rye and sugar with a slight hint of smoke.

Taste   Caramel and rye, a mixture of sweet and dry on the tongue with a short, light smoke finish.

CROWN ROYAL

Canada

Gimli Distillery
Gimli, Manitoba R0C 1B0
Tel: +1 204 642 5123
www.crownroyal.com

OWNERS: DIAGEO

BLEND FIRST LAUNCHED: 1939

VISITOR CENTER: No

The Crown Royal brand was first launched in Canada in 1939 to commemorate the visit of King George VI and Queen Elizabeth. It remained very much a local brand until 1965 when it was first launched in the United States.

The Crown Royal range was expanded in 1992 with the introduction of Crown Royal Special Reserve and more recently with Crown Royal XR. All three expressions I tasted were presented in decorated glass bottles presented in fabric bags tied with gold cord.

CROWN ROYAL FINE DE LUXE BLENDED CANADIAN WHISKY 40% (80°) LOT 5348

Color   Warm coppery gold.

Nose   Vanilla, honey, smooth grain notes.

Taste   Golden syrup with raisins and a spiced oak dry finish.

CROWN ROYAL SPECIAL RESERVE A RARE BLEND OF THE FINEST CANADIAN WHISKIES 40% (80°) LOT 6165

Color   Amber gold.

Nose   An intense complex nose with warm spice and hints of ginger, vanilla and burned grain.

Taste   Creamy sweetness and rye intermingling wrapped around cherries in chocolate and an oaky finish.

CROWN ROYAL XR RARE EXQUISITELY BLENDED WITH A RARE BATCH OF CANADIAN WHISKY 40% (80°) BOTTLE NO AA8787

Color   Warm amber with coppery red glints.

Nose   Rye is the first note with vanilla, apples ripening in the sun, and a hint of tangerine.

Taste   Balanced smooth fills the mouth with acacia honey notes and a bittersweet orange finish.

GEORGE DICKEL

USA

Cascade Distillery
1950 Cascade Hollow Road, Tullahoma, TN 37388
Tel: +1 931 857 3124
www.dickel.com

OWNERS: DIAGEO

COMPANY FOUNDED: 1870

VISITOR CENTER: YES

George A. Dickel founded his distillery in 1870 close to the Cascade Springs on the edge of the Cumberland Plateau situated between Nashville and Chattanooga. George created his whisky in small batches and soon realized that winter whisky was smoother than that produced in the summer. George's whisky is still chilled before maturation. Observant readers will notice that I have written George's whisky without the "e" traditionally used by American distillers. "George Dickel declared that because his whisky was as smooth as the finest Scotch, he would always spell the "whiskey" in George Dickel Tennessee Whisky without an "e," in keeping with the Scotch whisky tradition."

Visitors to Cascade Hollow will discover not just a great visitor center but also a post office – the only one in a distillery in the U.S.

There are several expressions of George Dickel including George Dickel Superior No 12 and George Dickel Barrel Select where the casks used are chosen by Master Distiller, John Lunn.

GEORGE DICKEL SUPERIOR NO 12 45% (90°)

Color   Warm summer gold.

Nose   A big nose with heavy floral notes, rye, caramel, and vanilla.

Taste   Rye gives this a warm bodied bite, then there is a smoother dry taste with crisp finish.

**GEORGE DICKEL BARREL SELECT 43% (86°)
BOTTLED 2006 CHARCOAL MELLOWED &
DOUBLE DISTILLED**

Color   Warm golden copper.

Nose   Rye, chestnut honey, burned toast, vanilla.

Taste   Initial burned caramel, licorice, then fills the mouth with toffee apples, warm cinnamon, and custard cream and a dry bittersweet finish.

GLENORA

Canada

Glenora Distillery
Route 19/Ceilidh Trail, Glenville, Cape Breton, Nova Scotia
Tel: +1 800 839 0491
www.glenoradistillery.com

OWNERS: GLENORA DISTILLERY COMPANY

FOUNDED: 1990

VISITOR CENTER: YES

G lenora is Canada's major single malt whisky. To my knowledge there is only one other — Okanagan Long Wood.

Bruce Jardine of Glenville, Cape Breton dreamed of building a Scottish style distillery in Cape Breton. Bruce began his distillery in 1986 and with advice from Harry Cockburn, then of Morrison Bowmore, he found the right place near the MacLelland Brook. Jardine researched whisky distillation, spending time in Scotland, and also sought Canadian investors for his new venture. The first whisky sold by his company was in fact purchased from Bowmore and bottled as Kenloch. This meant that the distillery had some stock to sell while the first spirits were maturing.

The distillery was built in 1990 and is a long low building with a traditional kiln. The whisky is produced in the traditional way with only barley, yeast, and water. The distillery copper pot stills were built by Forsyth's of Scotland.

For the early Scottish settlers this area of Nova Scotia reminded them of home, and the Gaelic traditions, language, and music live on at the distillery. Over 10,000 visitors come to Glenora every year, and some of them stay in the distillery inn so that they can immerse themselves in the ambiance, with daily ceilidhs from July to October.

Glen Breton Rare Canadian Single Malt Whisky shows no age on the bottle. There is also a Glenora 1990 14 year old Single Cask bottling available.

GLEN BRETON RARE 43% (86°)
(Tasting notes were provided by the distillery.)

Color Golden amber.

Nose Butterscotch, heather, honey, and ground ginger.

Taste Creamy with a good flow of toasty wood, almond, and caramel with a rounded, lingering, faintly sweet, merest whisper of peat finish.

HEAVEN HILL

USA

Heaven Hill Distillers, Bourbon Heritage Center
1311 Gilkey Run Road, Bardstown, KY 40004
Tel: +1 502 337 1000
www.heaven-hill.com

FOUNDED: 1934

OWNERS: HEAVEN HILL DISTILLERS

VISITOR CENTER: YES

Heaven Hill distillery was born in 1934 after Prohibition, during the depression in the United States. A group of Bourbon whiskey makers sought financial support from the Shapira brothers and the Old Heaven Hill Springs Distillery was built. Originally the Shapira family simply financed the project, but several years later became sole owners of the new venture.

After World War II the company started to create different bottlings and the business grew. In 1986, along with other Bourbon distillers, Heaven Hill started looking at small batch Bourbons. Their first release was an Elijah Craig 12 year old whiskey. Elijah was a Baptist minister and farmer who was distilling in the late eighteenth century. The company now markets a wide range of special expressions including Evan Williams (celebrating a distillery founded in 1783), Henry McKenna, Fighting Cock, Old Fitzgerald, Cabin Still, and Echo Spring.

In 1996 however, disaster struck in a severe storm; lightning hit the distillery and burning alcohol ran everywhere. The original distillery was converted into a visitor center and Heaven Hill acquired the Bernheim distillery in Louisville in 1999.

Distillation is now centered on Louisville. The master distiller is Craig Beam, who joined the company in 1982 and follows in the steps of his father Parker, grandfather Earl, and great-great uncle Harry.

ELIJAH CRAIG SINGLE BARREL 18 YEAR OLD
45% (90°)

Color Warm copper.

Nose Satisfying full aromas, rich fruit cake with caramel, vanilla, and toasted coconut.

Taste Full bodied with burned caramel, pineapple, dark chocolate, and rye with a lingering, slightly dry finish.

EVAN WILLIAMS BLACK 43% (86°)

Color Bright amber.

Nose Pear drops, aniseed balls with hints of leather and smoke.

Taste Creamy, medium bodied with honey and spice, fills the mouth with grain notes and a hint of bitterness in the long sweet finish.

JACK DANIEL'S

USA

Jack Daniel's Distillery
280 Lynchburg Hwy, Lynchburg, TN 37352
Tel: +1 615 759 6180
www.jackdaniels.com

OWNERS: BROWN FORMAN

FOUNDED: 1863

VISITOR CENTER: YES

Jasper (Jack) Newton Daniel was born in 1850, one of 13 children and from the age of seven Jack worked for Dan Call, a Lutheran Minister and part-time distillery owner. Dan's distillery was situated on the Louise River and young Jack appears to have been fascinated by the art of distilling, for when Dan decided to stop making whiskey, he sold the pot still to Jack.

So at the age of 12 we find Jack trying to make the perfect whiskey. His research took him until 1866 when he was happy with his refining or mellowing process which involves passing the new spirit through a large container filled with 10 feet (3 meters) of sugar maple charcoal. This adds aroma and taste and refines the new spirit. On his twenty-first birthday Jack went out and bought himself his trademark outfit, a hat and knee length coat, which he wore until he died. Jack's death was apparently as a result of an accident in the office. Jack arrived one morning in 1905 and couldn't remember the combination to the safe, so he kicked it and badly injured his toe. He died from blood poisoning in 1911. Jack had many "lady friends," but never married so the distillery was inherited by his nephew, Lem Motlow. There are chairs next to Jack's grave so that his friends could sit nearby and gossip.

Today, Lynchburg Tennessee is a quiet town with just 361 people, and many of them work for Jack Daniel's. The master distiller is Jimmy Bedford.

JACK DANIEL'S OLD NO 7 TENNESSEE WHISKEY
40% (80°)

Color   Warm mellow gold.

Nose   Rounded with a distinctive slick, caramel, dried apricots, and rye rawness aroma.

Taste   Caramel, spice, rye sharpness, charcoal smoke, medium-bodied with a warm finish.

JIM BEAM

USA

Jim Beam American Outpost
149 Happy Hollow Road, Clermont, KY 40110
Tel: +1 502 543 9877
www.jimbeam.com

JIM BEAM KENTUCKY STRAIGHT BOURBON
40% (80°)

Color   Pale copper gold.

Nose   Light and flowery with a hint of oak.

Taste   Rounded, mellow yet light on the tongue
with oak finish.

OWNERS: BEAM GLOBAL SPIRITS & WINE

FOUNDED: 1795

VISITOR CENTER: YES

Jim Beam is synonymous everywhere with the name of Bourbon, and Jim Beam four year old is one of the world's 20 top-selling spirits.

Jim Beam distillery was founded in 1795 by Jacob Beam, whose family had emigrated to America in the early 1700s from Germany. In the early 1800s, David Beam constructed the Clear Springs distillery, not far from the present site in Clermont. It was David's son, Jim, who built Clermont Distillery in 1933 at the end of Prohibition. It took him just 120 days to construct the distillery.

Jim's son Jeremiah took over the distillery in 1947, and in 1960 his grandson Booker Noe became Master Distiller. Today that title belongs to his son Frederick Booker Noe III who is the seventh member of the Beam family to run the distillery. The whiskey is still made to the original recipe, which is carefully preserved by Jim Beam's family.

Jim Beam is bottled at 40% (80°) and also as Jim Beam Black eight year 43% (86°), Jim Beam Rye, Beam's Choice, and Jim Beam 7-year.

In addition the distillery creates a series of small batch Bourbons which include Knob Creek, Booker's, Basil Hayden, and Baker's. Booker Noe, Jim Beam's grandson, is quoted as saying, "Sipping a small batch Bourbon is like tasting the past. This is Bourbon the way it used to be, the way it was meant to be." There is no doubt that these Bourbons are different and whiskey lovers should try them when the opportunity arises.

MAKER'S MARK

USA

Maker's Mark Distillery
3350 Burks Spring Road, Loretto, KY 40037
Tel: +1 270 865 2099
www.makersmark.com

OWNERS: BEAM GLOBAL SPIRITS & WINE

FOUNDED: 1840

VISITOR CENTER: YES

In 1780, Robert Samuels settled in Kentucky and may well have started making whisky as so many farmers had done in Scotland and Ireland before him. It was not until 1840 that T. W. Samuels started distilling in larger quantities; however, the first commercial distillery was not built until 1894. The next stage in the distillery's history shows that in 1943 Bill Samuels left the distillery and burned his family's old recipe. He believed that he must create a smoother recipe of his own to combat the increasing popularity of Scotch and Canadian whiskies over Bourbon.

The recipe he created uses red winter wheat, which comes from local farms, and no rye. The proportions are 70% maize (corn), 14% wheat, and 16% malted barley. The bottle for the new whisky was designed by Bill's wife. The design includes an "S" for "Samuels," IV for the fact that Bill Samuels Sr. was the fourth generation, and a star for the Star Hill Farm where Maker's Mark is produced. Bottles are hand dipped in red wax, which makes them stand out from the crowd. And, just to make sure that everyone realizes that Maker's Mark is different, the label shows the word "Whisky" and not "Whiskey" as more usually associated with American brands. The first bottles of Maker's Mark were sold in 1958.

Bottling runs use batches of less than 19 barrels, which have normally matured for six years in the company's warehouses. Bottlings are at various strengths usually 50.5% (101°) or 45% (90°).

MAKER'S MARK 45% (90°)

Color   Rich copper gold.

Nose   Warm, rich with spice and oak.

Taste   Lighter on the palate than you might expect at first, then sweetness and malt flavors fill the mouth. A short, crisp finish.

SEAGRAM'S

Canada

www.vowhisky.com / www.seagram7.com

OWNERS: SEAGRAM

COMPANY FOUNDED: 1857

BRAND FIRST LAUNCHED: 1919

Samuel Bronfman of Seagram's built his first new La Salle distillery near Montreal, Canada, in 1924. This was linked with the family's original Waterloo, Ontario distillery which dated back to 1857. The company also had distilleries in Amhertsburg, Ontario, and Beaupre in Quebec. It is no coincidence that Seagram's grew during Prohibition in the United States, and only a small percentage of the whisky produced was actually sold in Canada. By World War II Seagram's was the largest alcoholic distiller in North America.

Samuel believed that whisky should be enjoyed by everyone and an early advertisement read. "We who make whisky say Drink Moderately. The real enjoyment whisky can add to the pleasure of gracious living is possible only to the man who drinks good whisky and drinks moderately. Whisky cannot take the place of milk, bread, or meat. The pleasure which good whisky offers is definitely a luxury."

Writing in the 1970s Bronfman described how the company's fortunes spread geographically to include the Gimli Distillery, which is placed almost in the middle of Canada on the shores of Lake Winnipeg. By spreading his distilleries across Canada, he was able to provide whisky to a vast sector of the population.

There are various Seagram blends available including Seagram's Seven 7 Crown, which was created six months after the repeal of Prohibition.

SEAGRAM'S VO CANADIAN WHISKY A BLEND 40% (80°)

Color   Warm honey gold.

Nose   Rye, fermented grape juice, and burned caramel.

Taste   This is a relatively young blend (4 years old, I believe) with raw edges, with plenty of rye intensity.

SEAGRAM'S VO GOLD CANADIAN WHISKY A BLEND 8 YEARS OLD 40% (80°)

Color   Medium amber with gold reflectance.

Nose   Caramelized apples and oranges, grain and rye, with Turkish delight.

Taste   The additional years have added smoothness to the blend, honey, rye bite, and a full bodied finish.

WOODFORD RESERVE

USA

Woodford Reserve Distillery
7855 McCracken Pike, Versailles, KY 40383
Tel: +1 859 879 1812
www.woodfordreserve.com

OWNERS: BROWN FORMAN

COMPANY FOUNDED: 1800S

VISITOR CENTER: YES

The distillery was founded in the 1800s by Oscar Pepper with his manager James Crow. Woodford Reserve is distilled at the Labrot & Graham distillery.

The company has produced special official bottlings for the Kentucky Derby since 1999. The most recent bottles have paintings by celebrated artists of winning horses or local scenes on them. These bottlings reflect the history and racing heritage of the Blue Grass region, where Woodford Reserve is created.

Woodford Reserve is a small-batch Bourbon, this means that only 180 bottles are produced at any one time. The casks are personally selected by the master distiller, Chris Morris. Chris recently said that he is trying to create the most authentic Bourbon whiskey; to get as close as possible to the Bourbon that drinkers would have been able to taste 100 years ago.

WOODFORD RESERVE DISTILLER'S SELECT BATCH 20 45.2% (90.4°)

Color	Warm copper gold.
Nose	Strong caramel and rye notes with hints of ripe fruit.
Taste	Rye is the first thing to emerge then waves of vanilla and honey cream.

OTHER AMERICAN & CANADIAN WHISKIES

USA

Today, the number of distilleries is greatly reduced from the glory days of American whiskey. However, there are some wonderful whiskeys (whiskies) being produced in the United States. Some key brands are listed separately in the following pages, but here is an overview of the current situation.

BOURBON DISTILLERIES CURRENTLY OPERATIONAL:

Barton, *Bardstown — Barton Brands*
Buffalo Trace, *Leestown, Frankfort — Sazerac*
Brown Forman, *Shively, Louisville — Brown Forman*
Four Roses, *Lawrenceburg - Kirin*
Heaven Hill/Bernheim Distillery — *Heaven Hill Distillers*
Jim Beam, Boston, and Clermont Distilleries — *Fortune Brands*
Woodford Reserve *(Labrot and Graham) near Millville — Brown-Forman*
Maker's Mark, *Loretto — Fortune Brands*
Wild Turkey, *Lawrenceburg — Pernod Ricard*

TENNESSEE DISTILLERIES CURRENTLY OPERATIONAL:
George Dickel — *Diageo*
Jack Daniel — *Brown Forman*

Additionally there are single malt rye whiskies, for example see Anchor Distillery, four grain whiskies, straight wheat whiskey, and corn whiskeys.

SINGLE MALT WHISKEYS
There are also several distilleries making single malt whiskeys and the number is growing, so the list below may be incomplete by the time you read this book.

CLEAR CREEK DISTILLERY USA
This distillery in Portland, Oregon produces a range of single malts under the name McCarthy's.

EDGEFIELD DISTILLERY USA
Another Portland distillery making Edgefield Distillery Hogshead single malt.

ST GEORGE DISTILLERY USA
St George's Distillery is based in San Francisco, California expressions include Single Malt and St. George Lot Nos.

STRANAHAN DISTILLERY USA
Stranahan from Denver in Colorado is certainly a new one on me. I look forward to tasting their single malt soon.

The American market is slightly confusing as distilleries market a wide range of brand names, especially when it comes to small batch Bourbons. I think it is rather like visiting a bakery, whereby using the basic ingredients of flour, sugar, eggs, and fat the baker will produce plain sponges, fruit cakes, gingerbreads, shortbreads and so on. So by using different recipes and changing the length of maturation time, distillers are able to recreate whiskeys which would otherwise have disappeared.

The names often refer to long closed distilleries or master distillers. In fact the names reflect the history of the country and bring back memories of frontiersmen and adventure. There are names such as Rebel Yell, Pikesville Straight Rye, Old Rip van Winkle, and Penny Packer Sour Mash; even Mark Twain has a whiskey named after him.

HERE ARE A FEW WHISKEYS OMITTED FROM THE PREVIOUS PAGES

ANCIENT AGE STRAIGHT KENTUCKY BOURBON (BUFFALO TRACE)
Distilling started on the site in Leestown in 1860 by the Blanton family. In the 1880s the distillery passed to Captain George T. Stagg. Ancient Age also sells Single Batch Bourbons, one celebrating Elmer T. Lee, distillery manager at Leestown from 1952 to 1980, others include **Hancock's Reserve**.

EARLY TIMES (BROWN-FORMAN)
This distillery was founded in 1860 and became part of the Brown-Forman group in 1923. During Prohibition, Early Times along with a few others was given a license to produce "medicinal whisky." In 1987 Early Times Mint Julep was adopted as the official drink of the Kentucky Derby.

FOUR ROSES (KIRIN)
Kentucky Straight Bourbon produced by Master Distiller, Jim Rutledge. The distillery looks more like a Spanish hacienda with its arched windows and painted façade. This is a whiskey available around the world and but not very often its home town. Four Roses is available in several expressions including unaged, Black Label, and Platinum with several Single Barrel bottlings.

OLD FORESTER KENTUCKY STRAIGHT BOURBON WHISKY (BROWN-FORMAN)

This is a whisky, not a whiskey, which featured in many Raymond Chandler stories as the favorite drink of gumshoes and hoodlums alike. Old Forester contains more rye than many whiskies and has a full bodied slightly sharp flavor which distinguishes it from traditional Bourbons.

SAZERAC RYE WHISKEY — THE SPIRIT OF NEW ORLEANS (SAZERAC)

Sazerac Rye Whiskey was relaunched after a 116 year absence in 2005. Sazerac is distilled at Buffalo Trace Distillery and has been maturing in oak casks since 1998. The first bottlings were made in a recreation of the original late 1800s packaging.

WILD TURKEY (PERNOD RICARD)

Wild Turkey owes its origin to the Austin Nichol Company, a firm of grocers, wine and spirit merchants founded in 1855, which mainly imported goods from Britain. During World War II the company was unable to obtain stocks from either Scotland or Ireland, so decided to try and source a local whiskey for its customers. Wild Turkey was made for Austin Nichol by various distilleries until 1971 when they bought their own. Earlier Wild Turkey whiskeys were a marriage of the distillery's own and others such as Ancient Age. Today the whiskey is only produced at Wild Turkey.

WILD TURKEY 8 YEARS OLD 43.4% (86.8°)

Color   Warm gold.

Nose   Toffee and caramel with hints of oak.

Taste   Full bodied and rounded on the tongue, a warm whiskey with a long smooth finish.

Canada

DISTILLERIES WHICH ARE STILL OPERATIONAL IN CANADA:

Alberta, *Calgary, Alberta*
Palliser, *Alberta*
Gimli, *Manitoba*
Canadian Mist, *Ontario*
Walkerville, *Ontario*
Kittling Ridge, *Ontario*
Valleyfield, *Ontario*
And Glenora, *Nova Scotia*, which is a single malt distillery and is featured separately in this chapter.

The Canadian whisky industry has declined since the nineteenth century when there were many distilleries. In certain countries, such as Scotland, the growth of the railroad led to the creation of new distilleries.

However in Canada the reverse is probably true, for the introduction of the railroad meant that it was no longer necessary to make whisky in every town as it could be easily shipped in from elsewhere. By the late 1860s the sight of long whisky trains was common. For example, Corby's special train stretched to almost half a mile in length, carrying 50,000 gallons of whisky.

The majority of Canadian whiskies are blends, but there are some exceptions. The Canadian market is a little confusing — well it is to me anyway! Company names such as Century, Carrington, and Hood River distillers remain and it is difficult to know who produces which brand. In the main section of this chapter I have featured whiskies which I have been able to taste, Crown Royal, Canadian Club, Seagram's 7, and VO. There are clearly many others available for you to try.

WELSH WHISKY

Wales is not a country which springs readily to mind when talking about whisky. However, some of the great whisky distillers of American came from Wales, such as Jack Daniels, Elijah Craig, and Evan Williams.

The story of Welsh whisky itself is, until now, not a successful one. Bala Distillery, which was built near Frongoch, North Wales in 1889 by the Welsh Whisky distillery Co Ltd was closed in 1900. There were several attempts to revive the name, most notably in 1974 when Dafydd Gittins launched his company in Breacon, which

bought Scotch whisky and rebottled it, after making some changes, as Welsh Whisky. The company went bankrupt following claims of misleading the public as to the whisky's origins but was resurrected by some businessmen who commissioned a still and took over the existing plant. This was a shortlived venture, which failed in 1997.

The present day Welsh Whisky Company was founded in 1998 and first started producing on September 11, 2000.

PENDERYN

Wales

Penderyn Distillery
Penderyn, Wales CF44 0SX
Tel: +44 1685 813300
www.welsh-whisky.co.uk

OWNERS: WELSH WHISKY COMPANY LTD

FOUNDED: 1998

VISITOR CENTER: YES

The creation of the Welsh Whisky Company in 1998 heralded the re-awakening of whisky distilling in Wales after nearly 100 years.

An attempt to start a company had been made in 1997. The company had a Faraday still and this was purchased along with other equipment. The unique Faraday still creates whisky in a totally different way, as it is a pot still and column still in one unit. The inventor was Dr. David Faraday, Professor of Distilling at the University of Surrey. (His great-great-grandfather was Michael Faraday, the eminent scientist.)

He still had yet to produce whisky and the company asked Dr. Jim Swan to assist with the project. He decided that the company should purchase the wash from Brain's Brewery in Cardiff and following his research, asked the brewers to provide the wash directly to the distillery without sterilization, which is usual in the brewing industry.

The new make is surprisingly sweet and malty on the nose and there is no fiery spirit feel in the mouth, just light pepper and cream. The spirit comes off the still at around 90% and is reduced to 63% before maturation. The whisky is matured in a mixture of ex-Bourbon barrels from the United States and Madeira and Oloroso Sherry casks. There are now many bottlings of Penderyn, but I give notes here of the first release.

PENDERYN 46% (92°)
(First released on St. David's Day, 1st March, 2004)

Color   Amber gold.

Nose   Light refreshing with warm Madeira notes, dried fruit and hazelnuts.

Taste   Creamy mouthfeel, tropical fruits, and vanilla.

OTHER WORLD DISTILLERIES

This list is by no means complete, as there are many distilleries around the world, but it gives you a flavor of where whisky is being produced. Many of these I have yet to visit, but I am heading for Australia at the end of 2007 so look forward to tasting some different whiskies there.

BAKERY HILL DISTILLERY   AUSTRALIA

www.bakeryhilldistillery.com.au

Throughout history, distilleries have been founded as the result of one man's passion. Here at Bakery Hill the passionate man is David Baker. The first spirit was produced in 2000 and had to be matured for at least two years before it could be called whisky in Australia. The first peated malts were produced using imported malt from the UK, but David is hoping to produce some Australian peated malt soon. There are three Bakery Hill bottlings, Classic and Peated matured in ex-Bourbon casks, and Double Wood a mixture of ex-Bourbon and French oak.

DYC   SPAIN

Founded in 1959 by Nicomedes Garcia to produce whisky for the home market. The company's headquarters sit at the foot of the Sierra de Guadarrama, an imposing range of snow-clad mountains outside the city of Segovia. The company distills over 5.1 million gallons (20 million liters) of alcohol a year. DyC, which was launched in 1963, is one of the world's top selling blended whiskies.

GLANN AR MOR   FRANCE

www.glannarmor.com

This distillery started life very much in "somebody's kitchen" in 1999 when a little whisky was distilled. This is being marketed as Taol Esa after three years. The new distillery took a little longer to build and the first spirits ran from the still in 2005. They are currently making their first spirits as both un-peated and peated (35/40ppmillion) single malts which will be matured in Bourbon and Sauterne barrels.

HEUBLEIN DISTILLERY   BRAZIL

DURFEE HALL MALT WHISKY

This is one of several distilleries in Brazil which produce a variety of single malts and blended whiskies for the Brazilian market. I haven't had the opportunity of tasting them, but my fellow whisky writer Jim Murray mentions a few in his *Whisky Bible* should you be interested in exploring the Brazilian world of whisky.

JAGDALE GROUP, BANGALORE   INDIA

www.amrutdistilleries.com

AMRUT

This distillery started producing its own malt whisky for its MaQintosh and other brands. Barley is grown in Punjab and Rajasthan and as whisky matures quickly in the Indian climate it is bottled young at approximately 4 years old. The company is selling two expressions overseas, a single malt and a cask strength single malt unaged.

KIRIN BREWERY   JAPAN

FUJI-GOTEMBA

Fuji-Gotemba is a Japanese distillery located 2,000 feet above sea level, in the lower foothills of Mount Fuji. The distillery was built in 1973 as a joint venture between Kirin Brewery Company, Seagrams, and Chivas Brothers. In 2002 Kirin Brewery took control and the first single malt whiskies were released. Before then the majority of the distillery's production was destined for blended whiskies.

MCDOWELL'S   INDIA

McDowell's head office (the distillery is part of the UB group) is in Bangalore, but the distillery is in Goa, which is one of the most romantic settings.

MCDOWELL'S OAK MATURED SINGLE MALT WHISKY UNAGED 42.8% (75°)

Color   Pale summer gold.

Nose   Smoky, malt, green oak, grassy.

Taste   Dry bitter almonds, unripe apples with a hint of honey. With water the flavors expand and become sweeter. A dry finish.

MACKMYRA   SWEDEN

www.mackmyra.se

MACKMYRA SVENSK WHISKY

Established in 1999 using locally grown barley. Latest bottling I have seen is Preludium 03 matured in Bourbon casks and finished in Sherry, released in 2003 using casks filled from 1999–2003, 52.2%. I tasted this at the Groningen Whisky Festival (Holland) in February 2007. The nose is still spirity with a clean grain under-note with smoke. On the mouth there's smoke, slight sharp engine oiliness, with hints of cream and vanilla.

MERCIAN   JAPAN

KARUIZAWA
There are nine whisky distilleries in Japan, details of
Fuji-Gotemba are shown above and information on
Hakushu, Nikka, Yamazaki, and Yoichi are given in
the main part of this chapter. Mercian is the major
importer of Gonzalez Byass Sherry — as a result 90%
of the distillery's production is matured in Sherry
casks. This is a small distillery producing a wide
range of single cask bottlings as well as traditional
15, 17, and 21 year old expressions.

MILFORD   NEW ZEALAND
www.milfordwhisky.co.nz
Not a distillery, but a single malt, as Preston Associates
of Tarranga have purchased the last stocks of the
Willowbank Distillery in Dunedin from Seagram's who
marketed the whisky as Lammerlaw. They are currently
bottling Milford at 10, 12, and 15 years. The company
hopes to build its own distillery at Nevis Bluff on the
Kawaru River near Queenstown very soon.

MUREE BREWERY LTD   PAKISTAN
www.murreebrewery.com
They started brewing and distilling here in 1850 to
supply the British who missed the beer, whisky, and
other spirits they were used to at home. The brewery
still exists despite Pakistan being a Muslim country.
The reason being that when Pakistan was created, the
rights of the non-Muslim minorities were protected
and this included distilling and drinking alcohol.

Much of the distillery was damaged in a fire during
Partition, but parts of the original buildings still
exist. It has wash stills built outside in the open air
and cellars beneath the ground where the whisky
matures. This stops the whisky maturing too quickly
in the hot climate. Muree is bottled at 3, 8, and
12 years old. Muree is not sold outside Pakistan.

JAMES SEDGWICK DISTILLERY   S.AFRICA

THREE SHIPS 10 YEAR OLD
This distillery also produces a range of blends using
South African and Scotch Whisky.

SLYRS   GERMANY
www.slyrs.com
Slyrs produced their first Bayerische Oberland Malz
Whisky in 1999. The company has been producing
brandy and other spirits since 1928. Slyrs released
the 1999 distillation in 2002 and will continue to
release other bottlings at 3 years old.

SMALL CONCERN DISTILLERY   AUS/TAS

Cradle Mountain Pure Tasmanian Malt.

SOUTHERN DISTILLERIES   NEW ZEALAND
www.hokonuiwhiskey.com
Peter Wheeler and Malcolm Willmott have been
running their own boutique distilleries for some
25 years. They have recently got together to start
marketing various brands. Their single malt is The
Coaster which is matured in ex-Bourbon casks from Jim
Beam. They also market a blend, The Mackenzie. They
have also resurrected Murdoch McRaes original 1892
recipe for moonshine. Moonshine or illegal whisky was
produced in New Zealand from 1850 and only stopped
a century later when the last moonshiner was
prosecuted. The story of the McRaes is on the website
and makes fascinating reading. It is clear that the
McRaes were simply doing what their forefathers had
been doing in Scotland. The Moonshine recipe is
bottled as Hokonui and there is also a Hokonui liqueur
which is made with Southland manuka honey and mint.

TASMAN DISTILLERY   AUS/TAS

This distillery produces Great Outback Rare Old
Australian Single Malt Whisky.

TASMANIAN DISTILLERY   AUS/TAS

Brand names for their single malts are Old Hobart
and Sullivan's Cove.

TEERENPELI BREWERY
& DISTILLERY COMPANY   FINLAND
www.teerenpeli.com
The brewery was founded in 1995 and the small
distillery was established in 2002 using a Scottish
pot still. The company uses only local Finnish barley.
A limited bottling was released in 2005 after three
years, but the company wishes to mature the single
malt for longer and the next bottlings are not
anticipated before 2010.

VALLEY DISTILLERY   THE NETHERLANDS

A recent addition to the Dutch whisky market, there
are a few boutique distilleries springing up in the
Netherlands. Valley Single Malt Spirit was launched
at the Groningen Whisky Festival in February 2007.
It is matured in small casks.

WARENGHEM DISTILLERY   FRANCE
www.distillerie-warenghem.com

ARMORIK
Warenghem was founded in 1900 by Leon
Warenghem. The company distils a large number
of spirits and liqueurs, but it wasn't until 1994 that
their first whisky Armorik was produced.

Armorik is available as a single malt bottled at
about 5 years, but with no age shown and also as a
blend. The company sells 1 million bottles of whisky
annually around the world.

SPECIALTY BOTTLERS

SPECIALTY BOTTLERS

The ever-increasing interest in whisky around the world has led to many specialty bottlings. On the following pages, I give details of a few independent bottlers, many of whom have been in business for a very long time and have made a significant contribution to the growth in whisky sales around the world. This list is by no means definitive. For example, I have omitted companies such as Murray McDavid, Adelphi, Blackadder, and Dewar Rattray and I trust they will all accept my apologies as space is limited.

In addition to these specialty bottlers there are also a large independent whisky stores around the world. Many of the key players have launched their own bottlings and blends. These are worth getting to know, as their encyclopedic knowledge will help you discover the world of whisky and introduce you to new single malt expressions and blends. In the UK these include The Vintage House, 42 Old Compton Street, London, and Royal Mile

Whiskies, which has branches in Scotland and London. In France the leading player is La Maison du Whisky, with its main branch at 20 Rue d'Anjou, 75008 Paris — this has become a place of pilgrimage for French whisky drinkers since 1968. The company opened a store on Réunion Island in October 2002 and another in Singapore in July 2006.

In the Netherlands whisky drinkers are spoiled for choice with retailers such as Gall & Gall, Whiskyslijterij de Koning, and Whisky-en Wijhandel Verhaar.

In the United States whiskey connoisseurs will be rewarded by a visit to Park Avenue Liquors in New York City, Sam's Wines & Spirits in Chicago, and Sigel's Liquors in Dallas among many others.

The leading whisky journals in your country will guide you to the nearest specialty retailer who will certainly have some of the bottlings described in the following pages, although the exact expression I have provided tasting notes for may no longer be available.

ANGUS DUNDEE DISTILLERS PLC

United Kingdom

20-21 Cato Street,
London W1H 5JQ
Tel: +44 20 7569 2000
www.angusdundee.co.uk

COMPANY FOUNDED: 1950S

Angus Dundee is an independent, family-owned company founded over 50 years ago. The company has built up a wide portfolio of Scotch whisky stocks up to 40 years of age. Whiskies are available either bottled in Scotland or shipped overseas for bottling locally. The company sells to more than 70 countries and is responsible for 5 percent of total Scotch Whisky exports. Additionally, the company deals in gin and vodka.

Angus Dundee Distillers also own Tomintoul distillery (page 81) and Glencadam distillery (page 53).

As independent bottlers, Angus Dundee Distillers has a wide product range. Angus Dundee is a blend bottled as a standard unaged, a 12 year old, and as Old Dundee pure malt, which is a special bottling of 25 different single malts. The James Parker range also has two blends, a standard unaged and a 12 year old. The Scottish Royal series includes two different blended whiskies. The company also markets Mackillops Choice, a range of single cask bottlings drawn from the company's own stocks.

Angus Dundee also produces for customer's own brands.

BERRY BROS & RUDD

United Kingdom

3 St James's Street,
St James's, London SW1A 1EG
Tel: +44 870 900 4300
www.bbr.com

COMPANY FOUNDED: 1698

erry Bros & Rudd started life in Pickering Place, which is a small square behind 3 St. James's Street. The business pre-dates the naming of the square, as in 1698 the Widow Bourne started a grocer's store on the same site. Outside Berry Bros & Rudd's door there is a sign representing a coffee mill which dates from Widow Bourne's time. In 1731 William Pickering leased a building to trade as an "Italian warehouse" or grocers and arms painting and heraldic furnishing suppliers. He died in 1734 and his widow Elizabeth took over the business. She soon stopped the heraldic side of the business and the grocery grew to sell spices, tobacco, snuff, teas, and coffees. Since 1760 the company has been selling wines and spirits to the British Royal family.

There is a plaque in the narrow walkway between St. James's Street into Pickering Place which commemorates the fact that the government of Texas had their legation offices here from 1842–1845.

Today, Berry Bros & Rudd continue to sell fine wines and spirits. Doug McIvor is Spirits Manager & Buyer for Berry Bros & Rudd. His philosophy is "Never to bottle anything I would not enjoy drinking myself." His selection criteria must be the right one for not only are the customers happy but Berry Bros was voted *Whisky Magazine*'s Retailer with a Single Outlet of the Year, in 2006.

Blue Hanger blended malt has been sold since the early 1900s and celebrates one of the company's best customer's, Lord Coleraine, William "Blue" Hanger.

BERRY'S OWN SELECTION GLENLIVET 1974 CASK 3203 46% (92°)

Color	Pale summer gold.
Nose	Warm apricots, light honey, vanilla, and smoke.
Taste	In the mouth a velvety feel with subtle layers of smoke, honey, and citrus, with a soft, dry finish.

CADENHEAD'S

United Kingdom

83 Longrow, Campbeltown,
Argyll PA28 6EX
Tel: +44 1568 554258
www.wmcadenhead.com

COMPANY FOUNDED: 1842

Cadenhead's started in 1842 in the Netherkirkgate in Aberdeen and remained in the same premises for 130 years. George Duncan set up business as a vintner and whisky distillery agent. In 1858 his brother-in-law William Cadenhead joined the business and on George's death, William took over the company and changed the name. William was succeeded in 1904 by his nephew Robert Duthie. Robert was a shy man, very different to his uncle who had become very well known in the community. However, Robert was responsible for developing the company's key brands, single malt Scotch Whisky and Demerara Rum, and he built up Cadenhead's whisky portfolio.

Robert was killed by a tram on his way to discuss the company's financial problems in 1931 in the middle of the depression. Duthie was a bachelor and he left the business to his two sisters who knew absolutely nothing about business, but wanted Cadenhead's to survive. They put a long-serving employee, Ann Oliver, in charge. However, her administration skills were severely lacking, and in time the Trustees forced her to retire and the business was put up for sale. The warehouses and cellars were full of stock, but there were no records. Christie's, the auctioneers, were asked to sell the entire stock; and the sale on October 3–4, 1972 in London was the largest sale of wines and spirits ever held in the UK. The catalog ran to 167 pages. The sale was so successful that the amount raised exceeded the company's liabilities. Today the company has branches in the UK and Europe.

COMPASS BOX

United Kingdom

Compass Box Delicious Whisky Ltd,
Chiswick Studios, 9 Power Road, London W4 5PY
Tel: +44 20 8995 0899
www.compassboxwhisky.com

COMPANY FOUNDED: 2000

John Glaser founded Compass Box in 2000 after a successful career as Global Marketing Director for Johnnie Walker. John is passionate about whisky as you will see from his website. He describes what he does as follows, "We work like fine wine negociants, choosing individual casks of whiskies from different distilleries that offer complementary sets of flavors. We then blend these casks in small batches to make our proprietary whiskies."

The aim of Compass Box is to do things just a little bit differently by creating individual high quality whiskies in distinctive bottles, which will appeal especially to younger drinkers. John is inspired by the original blenders, people like George Ballantine, William Teacher, and the Chivas Brothers who pioneered the fine art of blending. They not only founded proprietary brands but also created small batches for their more affluent clients. And that's what John does today.

At the time of writing the range includes the blends on the right and Orangerie, an orange and whisky spice infusion.

OAK CROSS 43% (86°)
A blended malt whisky, some of which undergoes secondary maturation in new oak casks with French heads and American bodies.

Color   Pale gold.

Nose   Mown grass, barley malt.

Taste   Malt sweetness on the nose is replicated in the mouth, whipped vanilla ice cream with spiced apple and pears. Light spicy finish.

ASYLA 43% (86°)
A blend of grain and malt whisky.

Color   Light warm gold.

Nose   Think of walks in beech woods in the summer with sunlight on still sunlit ponds.

Taste   Blossoms, vanilla, a warm, well rounded mouthfeel with an interplay between the malt and grain whiskies lingering on the tongue.

PEAT MONSTER 46% (92°)
A blend of Islay and mainland single malts.

Color   Light gold.

Nose   Peat smoke wrapped in malt, currants and spice – plum pudding at the Gentlemen's Club.

Taste   Rich, warm bodied with plenty of smoke, and the other elements on the nose coming through with a honeyed mouthfeel and a lingering finish.

COMPASS BOX
WHISKY COMPANY

DOUGLAS LAING & CO LTD

United Kingdom

Douglas House,
18 Lynedoch Crescent, Glasgow G3 6EQ
Tel: +44 141 333 9242
www.douglaslaing.com

COMPANY FOUNDED: 1950

Douglas Laing & Co was founded by Fred Douglas Laing to bottle and blend his own blends, The King of Scots and House of Peers.

The company grew through exports to countries such as Uganda and the Far East. Idi Amin of Uganda who had proclaimed himself King of Scotland in the 1970s was a good customer for The King of Scots brand. In the Far East the company sold, among others, the McGibbon range, a deluxe whisky packaged in miniature ceramic golf bags.

The company is now in the hands of Fred's two sons, Stewart and Fred. The company's website has affectionate portraits of the two brothers from which I quote:

"Our two old "dinosaurs" have fortunately surrounded themselves with bright, young, computer literates. Fred and Stewart hope the company, established by their father in 1950, does not change too drastically from their much preferred older and slower style of doing business. Our Malt and Blended Scotch Whiskies have rested and matured over many long years, awaiting your consumption. Please enjoy them at the same leisurely pace that they have waited for you."

This lighthearted home page must not be seen to detract from the seriousness with which the brothers approach their bottlings. The Old Malt Cask Series was launched in 1999 to promote some of the fine single malts laid down by their father over 50 years. Other malts are marketed under the Platinum and Provenance labels.

THE KING OF SCOTS BLEND 43% (86°)

Color: Ginger and spice with honey, nuts, and barley.

Nose: Light, nutty, and citric.

Taste: Spicy, dry, and lightly smoked.

PLATINUM PORT ELLEN 28 YEAR OLD
56.1% (112.2°)

Nose: Considerably overt early notes from 28 years in Sherry cask soften to offer an attractive, spicy, and macerated currant character full of warm, malty overtones with the anticipated oily, peaty, and typical Islay qualities.

Taste: Most of the aromas are replicated on the tongue via a big oily body, carrying a sweet almost honeyed palate full of fruit, peat, warm barley, mocha, and licorice. Big, still boldly smoked, peated with leather iodine and old soft leather finish.

DUNCAN TAYLOR & CO LTD

United Kingdom

4 Upperkirkgate,
Huntly, Aberdeenshire AB54 8JU
Tel: +44 1466 794055
www.dtcscotch.com

COMPANY FOUNDED: 1938

This award winning company sells a wide selection of whiskies which range in age from 6 to 18 years old. The bestselling range is Duncan Taylor, all single cask, unchillfiltered, no added coloring, single malt and single grain whiskies, aged from 8 to 18 years. This includes rare or premium whiskies, for example Springbank, Rosebank. Whisky Galore is the second best selling range and features malts from 10 to 18 years old, again bottled at 46%, unchillfiltered, and without added coloring.

A quick look at their website will let you know which bottlings are available at any one time. Their current bottling list includes Glenlivet Single Malts, ranging in age from 33 to 36 years old, and Glenrothes from 34 to 36 years old.

Their number one blend is Scottish Glory which sells around the world. There are also several other blends including Glendarroch 15 year old deluxe blend which sells in the United States, Japan, and Belgium.

Reflecting the keen interest in Islay whiskies at the moment, the company markets Big Smoke 40 and Big Smoke 60 Islay Malts and Auld Reekie 12 year old Islay Malt.

DUNCAN TAYLOR BIG SMOKE 40 ISLAY MALT SCOTCH WHISKY 40% (80°)
Launched end 2006 this is Islay Malt Whisky and is bottled at 40% and 60%.

Color   Pale straw.

Nose   Deep peat fire smoke, coal tar, wet leaves, sea salt.

Taste   Big smoke impact, barbecues, salt laden air with a slight hint of honey in the finish.

DUNCAN TAYLOR SCOTTISH GLORY BLENDED WHISKY 40% (80°)

Color   Pale honey gold.

Nose   Big malt, honey, floral.

Taste   Clean, honeyed, interplay of sweet malt and grain. A medium bodied well balanced blend.

DUNCAN TAYLOR AULD REEKIE 12 YEAR OLD ISLAY MALT WHISKY 46% (92°)
Auld Reekie is an old name for Edinburgh, and relates to the eighteenth century when factories and many illicit distilleries created so much smoke that the air was thick and polluted.

Color   Very pale straw.

Nose   Wet bonfires, malted barley, hints of lemon, and hot porridge.

Taste   Creamy smoke and honey with a long finish.

GORDON & MACPHAIL

United Kingdom

George House,
Boroughbriggs Road, Elgin IV30 1JY
Tel: +44 1343 545111
www.gordonandmacphail.com

COMPANY FOUNDED: 1895

Gordon & MacPhail are located in Elgin, a historical city in the north of Scotland. Elgin developed as a result of the prosperity bought to the area by large farms and distilleries — Corn Crain, Caul, Manbeen, Lesmurdie, Linkwood, and Miltonduff — only the latter two have survived.

The growth of Elgin brought prosperity to merchants operating in the city. On May 24, 1895 James Gordon and John MacPhail started a grocer's and wine and spirits merchant. James Gordon appears to have been the driving force.

The company grew and new distilleries were built in the area including Benriach, Glen Elgin, Coleburn, and Glen Moray. This period of growth was damaged by the collapse of the Pattison blending company which forced many distilleries and merchants to close. Gordon & MacPhail survived and continued to build up stocks of fine single malts.

In 1915 John MacPhail retired and John Urquhart who had been with the company for some time formed a new partnership with James Gordon. Unfortunately, only two weeks afterward, James Gordon died of a heart attack. Mrs Gordon carried on her husband's role as co-partner and John Urquhart set about developing the whisky side of the business.

In the 1930s and 1940s considerable stocks of fine malts were laid down and the Connoisseurs Choice range was launched; even though the fashion was for blends, and very few distilleries were selling their own single malts. The company is still very much a family firm and is owned by John Urquhart's descendants.

IAN MACLEOD & CO LTD

United Kingdom

*Russell House,
Dunnet Way, Broxburn EH52 5BU
Tel: +44 1506 852205
www.ianmacleod.com / www.smokehead.co.uk*

COMPANY FOUNDED: 1936

Ian MacLeod & Co Ltd is a leading light in the whisky industry with ranges sold throughout the world. The company was founded in 1936 by Leonard J Russell and the Chairman Peter Russell joined his father in 1956 as a whisky broker supplying companies with whiskies for their own blends. His son, Leonard, is now Managing Director of the company, which he joined in 1989.

Ian MacLeod & Co Ltd owns a wide range of brand names such as Isle of Skye Blended Scotch Whisky and London Hill Gin. The company purchased Glengoyne Distillery and Lang's Blended Scotch Whisky in 2003.

The ranges include Macleod's, 8 year old regional single malt Scotch whiskies bottled at 40%. Dun Bheagan, which includes 8 year old single malt Scotch whiskies, and the Dun Bheagan Vintage Malts, which are usually older. Both of the Dun Bheagan ranges are unchillfiltered and natural colored.

The Chieftain's range includes whiskies up to 50 years old, some are bottled at cask strength and some are finished in port, Sherry, or other casks.

DUN BHEAGAN CAOL ILA 10 YEAR OLD 43% (86°)

Color   Light hay.

Nose   Peat smoke punch, fusel oils.

Taste   Smoky, oily, expanding to honey and malt, warm burned caramel and smoke finish.

CHIEFTAIN'S IMPERIAL 24 YEAR OLD 46% (92°)

Color   Pale straw gold.

Nose   Light smoke, tobacco, honey, violets.

Taste   Delicate, light bodied, honey shortbread, malt, and peat smoke with a short light honey and smoke finish.

SIX ISLES BLENDED MALT 43% (86°)

Color   Very pale almost pale lime green.

Nose   Light peat, wafts of barley malt, passion fruit, and licorice.

Taste   Warm honeyed peat smoke, hints of caramel oranges, light cream mouthfeel. A long smoke filled finish with honey and vanilla. This is a very good blended island malt.

SMOKEHEAD ISLAY SINGLE MALT 43% (86°)

Color   Pale gold.

Nose   Sea salt, smoke bonfire, malt.

Taste   Smoke sensation fills the mouth, but soon rather sadly fades leaving light honey, citrus, short finish.

153

LOCH FYNE WHISKIES

United Kingdom

Inverary,
Argyll PA32 8UD
Tel: +44 1499 302219
www.lfw.co.uk

OWNERS: RICHARD JOYNSON, LOCH FYNE WHISKIES

COMPANY FOUNDED: 1992

Loch Fyne Whiskies is a favorite stopping point on the way to the Islay ferry. The owner Richard Joynson is an expert in the world of whisky and it is certainly worth visiting Loch Fyne Whiskies. He also has a slightly different approach, and visitors to Bruichladdich will remember Richard's tours describing "hamsters running around keeping the wheels going." And, if you want to keep up with what is going on in the world of whisky subscribe to his magazine the *Scotch Whisky Review*.

The serious side of Loch Fyne Whiskies is of course the whisky. Richard holds an extensive stock of single malts from standard expressions to rare bottlings. In addition the company markets its own Loch Fyne Blend, which was specially created by Professor Ronnie Martin, former Production Director of United Distillers. The label shows the Glendarroch Distillery (Glenfyne), which was built in 1831 on the Crinan Canal. The illustration shows how the distillery would have looked when Alfred Barnard visited it in 1885. The distillery closed in 1937 and there is nothing left of the buildings today.

The company also markets The Loch Fyne Liqueur a blend of 12 year old Scotch with natural chocolate, orange, and tangerine flavors.

THE LOCH FYNE BLEND 40% (80°)

Color   Light honey gold.

Nose   A hint of peat with honey, spice, and malt.

Taste   The peat on the nose is wrapped around with spice, malt, caramel, and a slightly bitter orange note.

PRABAN NA LINNE — THE GAELIC WHISKIES

United Kingdom

Eilean Iarmain,
Isle of Skye IV43 8GR
Tel: +44 1471 833496
www.gaelicwhisky.com

OWNERS: SIR IAIN NOBLE, PRABAN NA LINNE

COMPANY FOUNDED: 1976

Sir Iain Noble brings a different view to the marketing of Scotch malt whisky. Sir Iain is a banker and business entrepreneur who purchased a house on the Sleat Peninsula on Skye in 1972. He made up his mind to create employment on Skye and learn to speak Gaelic. "Without Gaelic, a door is always closed to you in the Hebrides."

Sir Iain's first whisky Te Bheag was chill filtered and bottled at 40% (80°). Nearly all standard bottlings from the major whisky companies are chill filtered before bottling. This means that many trace elements are removed, so that the whisky remains clear in the glass when water is added. The distillers believe that the majority of consumers prefer this to cloudy whisky. In the 1990s all that changed, as Sir Iain had tasted some early unchillfiltered whiskies and believed that they were simply that much better. So today, Praban na Linne has a range of unchillfiltered whiskies, which have won awards around the world. The original Te Bheag ("the little lady" or "wee dram") is still chill filtered. Sir Iain also states, (with his tongue slightly in his cheek, I presume), "that the Gaelic labelling greatly improves the flavour of the whisky."

The next ranges were MacNaMara Blended Scotch Whisky followed by Poit Dhubh ("illicit still" in Gaelic) Malt Scotch Whisky. Poit Dhubh Gaelic Malt Whisky is a blend of Islay and Speyside malts. In 2006 a Rum Finish MacNaMara Blended Scotch Whisky was launched, which is finished in Guyanan Rum casks.

POIT DHUBH 12 YEAR OLD 43% (86°)

Nose   Medium-bodied with firm dark smokiness, a touch of licorice, a slight hint of lime.

Taste   Medium sweet, rich with a good backbone of peatiness. Long, smooth, and smoky finish.

MACNAMARA RUM FINISH BLENDED SCOTCH WHISKY UNCHILLFILTERED 46% (92°)

Nose   Light, biscuitlike with a touch of sugared rum sweetness.

Taste   Fresh, smooth, slightly oily balanced by the sweetness from the rum, medium length, slightly creamy finish.

SIGNATORY VINTAGE SCOTCH WHISKY CO LTD

United Kingdom

Edradour Distillery
Pitlochry, Perthshire PH16 5JP
Tel: +44 1796 472095

1975 LINLITHGOW 51.7% (103.4°)

Color   Sunny gold.

Nose   Honeyed malt, fresh mown grass.

Taste   Light honey, oak, short finish.

OWNERS: SIGNATORY VINTAGE SCOTCH WHISKY CO LTD

COMPANY FOUNDED: 1988

Signatory was founded in 1988 by Andrew Symington. Andrew was brought up in Currie, Edinburgh and took an HND in hotel catering at Napier College in the city. He lists his interests as travel, fine wine, and dining. To this should be added a complete obsession with finding the very best casks of whisky. Starting the company was tough at first but slowly his determination to find whiskies for the connoisseur paid off, and today Signatory is one of the largest independent whisky bottlers. Signatory moved from its original headquarters in Edinburgh to new premises at the company's Edradour distillery in November 2007. This provides the company with purpose-built facilities including its own bottling line. The bottling line is semi-automated, but labels and packing are carried out by hand.

Why Signatory? Well, Andrew says that he thought he would "find someone famous to sign the labels for bottles produced from one single cask. The first cask we purchased was a cask of 1968 Glenlivet, which was sold long before we could find a famous person."

There are three key ranges, Signatory Cask Strength, Traditional Signatory 43% (86°), and Signatory unchillfiltered 46% (92°).

Andrew firmly believes that some of the older whiskies, such as sherried Speysides, can lose their original flavors and aromas when water is added, which is why so many are bottled at cask strength. All are unchillfiltered and natural in color with nothing added.

VERSAILLES DRANKEN

Netherlands

Lange Hezelstraat 76,
6511 CL Nijmegen
Tel: +31 24 323 2008
www.versaillesdranken.nl

OWNERS: CAECIL GERRITS

COMPANY FOUNDED: 1996

Versailles Dranken is a wine and spirits company in the Netherlands, which, like many similar businesses worldwide, market a wide variety of single and blended whiskies from around the globe. And like many of these companies, Caecil Gerrits has his own range of specialty bottlings. Versailles Dranken has its own whisky club as well, with frequent tastings and special events throughout the year.

In 2003 Caecil approached me and asked if I would work with him to create a range of single cask bottlings (right). The first collection was launched in November 2003 and included Rosebank Lowland 1990, Mortlach Speyside 1990 matured in a Sherry Butt, Bowmore Islay 1990, and Clynelish Highland 1990.

The collection was very well received and since then Versailles Dranken has bottled 10 more single casks. The latest was a special Caol Ila 1996, released to celebrate the 10th anniversary of Versailles Dranken in connection with a Peat Walk, which took place on the September 16, 2006. The seven Islay whisky distilleries participated, including distillery managers John Campbell from Laphroaig and Duncan McGillivray from Bruichladdich.

MANNOCHMORE 1984 UNCHILLFILTERED
46% (92°)

Color   Light copper gold.

Nose   Initially burned matches reflecting the Sherry finish, but as it opens out caramel, spice, and warm fruits.

Taste   A full bodied single malt with toffee, chocolate, and hints of tar. Then with just a little water, flavors of caramelized plum tart and custard. Dry, warm medium length finish with honeyed caramel, chocolate, coal, tar, and rubber.

CAOL ILA 1996 CASK STRENGTH
UNCHILLFILTERED 57.3% (114.6°)

Color   Straw yellow, slightly green, clear shiny light gold.

Nose   Explosion of peat, slightly apple fruitiness, hints of marshmallow, caramel, peat slowly disappears and lemony nose opens. With water, coconut notes.

Taste   Smoke on the tongue with oily honey sweetness. Well balanced, creamy filling the mouth with hints of fresh cut summer barley and licorice. Long, lingering peat, fruit flavors with honey, hints of licorice, and oak.

VINTAGE MALT WHISKY COMPANY

United Kingdom

2 Stewart Street,
Milngavie, Glasgow G62 6BW
Tel: +44 141 955 1700
www.vintagemaltwhisky.com

FINLAGGAN OLD RESERVE SINGLE ISLAY MALT 40% (80°)

Color   Pale gold.

Nose   Full bodied, burned caramel, candied orange, and a hint of smoke.

Taste   The mouth fills with peat smoke and then the burned caramel on the nose comes through. A long smoky, candied peel finish.

COMPANY FOUNDED: 1992

Brian Crook started working in the malt whisky industry in 1978 with Eadie Cairns & Company Ltd who owned Auchentoshan. In 1983 he joined Stanley P. Morrison Ltd, owners of Bowmore distillery. Just after his arrival they bought Auchentoshan, so he found himself back where he started. Brian became Sales Director of the company, which by then was called Morrison Bowmore. In 1992 he decided to leave and set up his own whisky company.

Brian and his wife Carol set up the Vintage Malt Whisky Company on April 1, 1992. The company has grown exponentially and their whiskies are now found in many countries around the world. By the end of 2006 they had exported 1.2 million bottles of malt whisky.

The company's key brands are Finlaggan, a single malt from Islay, and Glenalmond, a blended Highland Malt. The company also sells a range of Single Cask Bottlings under the name of Cooper's Choice, "dedicated to the men whose skills are an essential element in the maturation of malt whisky." Cooper's Choice single malts are chosen to reflect "the varied tastes and flavours to be found from the Eastern coastline, to the Highland valleys and all the way to the Western Isles."

Finlaggan has a drawing of a castle on the label. Finlaggan was where the Lord of the Isles ruled Scotland. Today, there is only a pile of stones so the drawing is a bit of fantasy. However, the whisky is definitely not, and is a good Islay dram worth seeking out in your local liquor store.

INDEX